The Morality Pill

The Ethics of Moral Enhancement

Matteo Galletti

Translated by
Steven Umbrello

Applied Ethics: From Bioethics to Environmental Ethics, vol. 5

The Morality Pill: The Ethics of Moral Enhancement
Matteo Galletti, trans. Steven Umbrello
ISBN 978-615-6696-40-3
Applied Ethics: from Bioethics to Environmental Ethics, vol. 5
ISSN 2630-8185
Responsible Publisher: Teodora C. Artimon
https://trivent-publishing.eu/45-applied-ethics

First published in English in 2025 by Trivent Publishing

Trivent Publishing
1119 Budapest, Etele ut 59-61
Hungary

For more information, visit our website: http://trivent-publishing.eu

APPLIED ETHICS:
FROM BIOETHICS TO ENVIRONMENTAL ETHICS

TABLE OF CONTENTS

TRANSLATOR'S FOREWORD

Steven Umbrello

I have been asked numerous times, given that this is not the first monograph I have taken upon myself to translate, "Why would you take the time to translate a book? It seems like so much work". It certainly is true that the translation of any work from its original language is a burdensome task; not only is the translator looking to remain faithful to the author's intent but stylistic changes will almost certainly be made to ensure that nothing is lost in translation. This is particularly true for philosophical treatises like the present volume. Philosophical nuance is predicated on the minutiae of language; thus, one must ensure that such is not painted over.

Given the work it takes, the real question is the "why" of translating a book. I met the author of this book, Matteo Galletti, at the Turin International Book Fair in the Spring of 2022, where Fandango, the original publisher of his volume, presented the first two books in their new *Icaro* book series. The first book, published by Maurizio Balistreri, explored the ethical issues of children's genome editing, a challenging and controversial topic. The second presented book was that of Galletti. The books in this *Icaro* series are intended to provide introductory and easily approachable philosophical issues to a general audience. Galletti's work, which explores moral bio-enhancement and the ethical issues surrounding it, has been widely disseminated in the anglophone world, albeit mainly at an academic level, making the rich philosophical debate hard to access by even interested novices. Galletti takes a wholly different approach to presenting the topic.

Written in an accessible and flowing style, Galletti presents the reader with timely and speculative examples of the world we live in and the one we may be heading to concerning augmenting our moral sensitivities with technology. The volume gives not only a foundational introduction to the ethical issues relating to these technologies and their applications but also a primer on moral theory as well, taking a look at the traditional ideas of utilitarianism, deontology, and virtue ethics. Interested readers on the topic need not approach the book with the requisite knowledge at hand; Galletti provides the philosophical and conceptual tools that any reader will need to broach this otherwise complex subject.

Bringing what is otherwise an engaging, approachable, and important topic to a general audience is no unimportant task. Given the absence of similar work in the English language, it was a no-brainer to take up the task of translating Galletti's work into the volume you now hold.

INTRODUCTION

Dilemmas. How to Morally Augment Humanity

"Violence is a horrible thing, you know? Furthermore, he is learning it. He learns it like this."

Alex is lying on a bed talking to a doctor: he is amazed that, for the first time, he feels nauseous when he violently watches violent videos. In the past, when he was an accomplice to violence, or even a direct perpetrator, he did not feel as bad as now. The doctor replies that this discomfort indicates an improvement in Alex's condition. In a healthy person, the normal response to violence is to feel nauseous and anxious. Alex's treatment is paying off, and the criminal is on the road to recovery.

It is a famous scene from Stanley Kubrick's *A Clockwork Orange* (1971), in which Alex and his group of companions move to England in an unknown future. The "droogs", as they call themselves, commit all kinds of violence: they steal, beat, rape and kill. Alex, however, is arrested and, after a period in prison, subjected to a radical re-education programme, the "Ludovico Technique", in which the subject is forced to take drugs and watch videos of violent scenes while tied to an armchair while an ophthalmic speculum is placed on his head to force him to keep his eyes open. The treatment aims to make Alex feel nauseous, painful, uncomfortable and disgusted by the violence in order to change his attitudes and behaviour. The effect of the substances administered, combined with graphic violence, is intended to 'correct' Alex's future actions and inhibit the urge to commit atrocities.

The themes of choice and freedom recur frequently in the film scenes. Part of the treatment protocol involves Alex listening to the works of Ludwig van Beethoven, his favourite musician, during sessions. Alex seems to rebel at one point: "It's not fair, it's not fair that I should feel ill when I hear lovely, lovely Ludwig van...". The doctor supervising the treatment replies: "You must take your chance, boy; the choice has been all yours". Alex desperately replies: "You needn't take it any further, sir. You've proved to me that all this ultraviolence and killing is wrong, wrong, terribly wrong. I've learned the lesson, sir. I've seen now what I haven't seen before. I'm cured, praise god! [But sir, misses, I see that it's wrong. It is wrong because it is against society and because everyone has the right to live and be happy without being tortured and knifed". The doctor did not believe him, and the treatment had to continue for another 15 days before Alex was released.

Alex had *freely* chosen to undergo this new treatment. In an earlier scene, the boy is seen in conversation with the prison chaplain in the library. Alex shows him the will to start the Ludovico treatment, but the priest is sceptical. This is an experimental treatment whose side effects and effectiveness have yet to be fully proven. Above all, he adds, it is not clear whether the new technique really can create "good" from a moral point of view because goodness is the result of choice and not of conditioning. The impossibility of choice takes away from the human being what distinguishes him from the rest of living beings: free will. Alex's reply is interesting: he does not care to understand the reasons or causes of goodness; he just *wants* to be good. That is, he is satisfied with manifesting the external characteristics of goodness, mainly as a means to be released from his imprisonment.

The concept is then reiterated by the chaplain, who speaks to the Minister of the Interior during a demonstration for the authorities, in which Alex's violent instincts are stopped by an attack of nausea, preventing him from hitting a man who verbally and physically assaults him, and forcing him to lick the sole of his shoe. After the Minister's speech on the effects of the Ludovico Technique, the Chaplain intervenes to emphasise the real reasons for Alex's reaction: "Choice! The boy has not a real choice, has he? Self-interest, and the fear of physical pain drove him to that grotesque act of self-abasement. The insincerity was clear to be seen. He ceases to be a wrongdoer. He also ceases to be a creature capable of moral choice".

Moreover, in return, the minister asks the man of the church to abandon the sophistry because what interests the public authorities are not the subtleties of ethics but the reduction of delinquency and the number of prisoners in prisons. Moral goodness is measured based on how the method works and its ability to affect people's behaviour: now Alex is a "good Christian", ready to turn the other cheek and nauseated at the idea of committing evil. It matters little if philosophers can judge him as lacking free will. Isn't collective prosperity more critical? From the point of view of "raison d'état", the sacrifice of a "metaphysical" characteristic such as free will is entirely admissible if it allows you to enjoy tangible goods such as public safety and well-being.

In *A Clockwork Orange*, many of the arguments concerning "moral improvement", that is, the set of techniques that make it possible to make individuals better, more just and more altruistic, recur, so much so that the scenes just mentioned have been used quite frequently in the philosophical debate (Hauskeller, 2017). The Ludovico Technique can be considered a form of "aversion therapy", that is, the induction of an unpleasant sensation in a subject when he or she performs an undesirable behaviour, thanks to a conditioning procedure. It is therefore an intervention that induces a particular feeling of physical disgust without reinforcing moral dispositions or moral reasoning. As we shall see, the forms of 'moral enhancement' that are generally discussed concern the creation or reinforcement of certain motivations, such as altruism and a sense of justice, or the strengthening of cognitive mechanisms that allow the acquisition of a better knowledge of what is right and wrong. Despite these differences, the criticisms raised by the chaplain are similar to those discussed in the case of the use of biotechnological means to enhance the moral sense of individuals.

In the first chapter, we will explore all the definitions necessary to understand what it means to enhance human beings and what it means to bio-enhance them morally. In addition to the definitions, we will describe the pharmacological, genetic and neurological interventions that some authors believe may be used in the future to enhance the moral capacities of human beings. But why do we need moral bio-enhancement? Essentially, as we will see at the end of the chapter it is seen as a faster and more effective means of achieving the goals set by traditional means such as education, critical reflection, and socialisation.

The second chapter explores the merits of moral bio-enhancement. What does the term "morality" mean? In the field of ethical reflection, it has been interpreted in different ways, and today the picture is further enriched by empirical data coming from studies on the biological basis of morality and moral psychology. These data create a kind of paradox: if on the one hand they strengthen the perspective of intervening in biological nature to modify morality, on the other hand they complicate the picture by suggesting the existence of different theories about what motivations and processes can be involved in morality. Because of this pluralism, perceptions of authentic moral bio-enhancement and judgments about which interventions are beneficial and effective also vary.

The third chapter addresses one of the main issues in the debate: the impact of moral bio-enhancement on human freedom. If these interventions lead people to behave morally, then they will be deprived of the freedom to choose evil voluntarily. But what kind of freedom is that? Is it wrong to lose it if the gain is a (potential) reduction in violence, wickedness, and injustice? This is essentially the question to which the chaplain and the minister in *A Clockwork Orange* give diametrically opposed answers. It is, therefore, important to clarify what we mean when we talk about freedom and what value can be attached to it.

The fourth chapter deals with the question of whether the reasons that have led some authors to believe that moral bio-enhancement is the only way out of the perilous situation in which humanity finds itself are genuine. Is moral progress impossible without bioenhancement? Finally, in the light of some of the ideas developed in the previous chapters, we will argue that acceptable bioenhancement enhances, or at least facilitates, the exercise of reflective capacities. We will give an example of how this can happen by analysing the use of some psychopharmaceuticals, such as those used to treat attention deficit hyperactivity disorder (ADHD).

Ultimately, the debate on moral bio-enhancement is useful for several reasons. First, it allows us to understand what biotechnological developments humanity can expect, and to think about possible responses to such developments. Second, it can help clarify what we mean when we say that human beings should be morally 'good' and 'just'. In this book we will not be able to answer all these questions. But we will try to clarify some basic issues, with the idea that a cautious but not entirely closed approach to moral bio-enhancement is reasonable at a time when there are more doubts than certainties.

CHAPTER 1

What is Moral Bio-enhancement?

What is Enhancement?

The human species has always sought to improve its activities by enhancing physical and mental characteristics. Eyeglasses allow us to see better, food supplements increase our nutrient intake, vaccines boost our immunity, and graphite rackets improve the performance of tennis players compared to wooden ones. In principle, any artefact that allows you to perform better than you did in the past can be considered a form of enhancement. However, looking carefully at the (partial) list of examples we have just given, you will see that not all enhancements are the same. Glasses or contact lenses improve a person's vision compared to the norm. People who are not nearsighted, presbyopic, visually impaired or colour blind do not need glasses and usually do not wear them. The situation is different when it comes to tools such as tennis rackets, made from materials that make it possible to give the instrument special shapes and lighter weights to improve control of the shots. In these cases, we are not discussing a defect compared to the average but rather an attempt to elevate the standard by giving all players more effective equipment.

The examples are endless. Some substances, generally used as therapies for established disorders, can improve the cognitive abilities of healthy people. University students often take methylphenidate to improve attention and study performance, as it can enhance memory, alertness, and motivation in people without cognitive disorders. Similarly, the psychostimulant modafinil can help develop greater cognitive control and focus (Colazato & Arntz, 2017; Colazato & Mourits, 2017; Westbrook et al., 2020). In the future, some believe that thanks to technologies such as CRISPR-Cas9, we may be able to modify genomes to obtain changes in the biological structure of somatic cells or human embryos, creating more robust, more powerful, faster or more disease-resistant individuals (Almeida & Diogo, 2019; Balistreri, 2022; Greely, 2021).

Therefore, we are not talking about interventions that 'normalise' cognitive characteristics, but about drugs and biological modifications that can increase performance above the average, helping people perform specific tasks more efficiently. We can therefore provisionally define enhancement in the following way:

> An intervention that uses medical and biological technologies to improve performance, appearance, or capabilities beyond what is necessary to achieve, maintain, or recover health.

This definition (Mehlman, Berg, Juengst, Kodish 2011, p. 31; Juengst and Moseley 2019, par. 1.1) seems to capture an intuitive aspect of enhancement, i.e. the crossing of a defined threshold thanks to the creation of individuals that go beyond the average, up to radical results (Agar 2010 and 2014). However, this definition seems unsatisfactory for several reasons.

1. The definition refers to a threshold above which the intervention can be defined as enhancement and below which the intervention aims to restore or maintain a state of health. This threshold essentially introduces a distinction between 'enhancement' and 'therapy', the descriptive and evaluative validity of which is highly controversial. Firstly, it is not clear whether it is possible to make this distinction, since any successful therapy is an enhancement of the human body, and both types of intervention aim to improve the well-being of the individual (The President's Council on Bioethics, 2003, pp. 13-16; Harris, 2007; Savluescu, Sandberg and Kahane, 2011). Moreover, this distinction is often proposed not only to find an acceptable way of descriptively diversifying the types of intervention, but also to formulate a moral judgement: while "therapies" fall within the set

of morally licit actions because their purpose is paradigmatically considered laudable, enhancements present themselves in at least a suspicious light. According to a moderate judgement, they are superfluous compared to the genuine necessity that characterises the therapies, because they try to satisfy artificial and inauthentic human needs. According to a more radical judgement, they express, more or less consciously, an attitude of arrogance, a mania for control, a convulsive and illogical search for perfection and overcoming the natural limits of human action (Sandel, 2008). It is doubtful, however, whether these arguments hit the mark (Balistreri, 2020). First, given the close relationship between therapies and enhancements and the 'mixed' nature of many interventions, the two types of intervention are not distinguished at the regulatory level. If they are effective, both are desirable and acceptable. Furthermore, viewing enhancements as an expression of Promethean hubris seems untenable. Those who wish to resort to enhancements may want to increase their potential opportunities and quality of life for themselves and future generations, without demonstrating arrogant intentions. Moreover, as noted above, human history is replete with continuous attempts to modify one's biological nature and to enhance one's abilities and performance (Buchanan, 2011, ch. 2). To rigidly accept the normative distinction between therapies and enhancements would be to reject all such actions as 'enhancements', and this judgement would seem largely counterintuitive. In fact, these attempts have often resulted in positive outcomes for humanity.

2. The introduction of the term "biomedical" limits the group of interventions to biological and medical techniques that can have performance-enhancing effects. Nevertheless, attending an excellent school or gym, repeated and systematic individual exercise and constant training can improve human performance by altering neural or physical structure. Although these methods also involve the use of technology (writing, memorising, physical training, etc.), they do not usually use the biomedical means offered by neuroscience, genetics or pharmacology. This point is critical, and again marks a divide between those who argue that there is substantial continuity between 'traditional' and biomedical means,

and those who stress the profound difference between the two methods (cf. Harris, 2007; Habermas, 2002, pp. 50-51, 84-85). In this case, the difference in position is also based on a different moral judgement of the instruments under consideration. The more an individual enhancement relies on means that directly modify human biological nature, the more suspect it appears from a moral point of view. This distinction seems problematic and cannot be taken for granted.

3. Third, the definition describes enhancement as any intervention that increases capacity or disposition. Sometimes one can enhance performance or improve an individual's well-being by subtracting or reducing a capacity or function. In certain situations and contexts, a person might perform better if certain emotions were dampened, or they might feel better if, for example, an intervention was used to reduce their ability to remember traumatic or painful events (think of the services provided by Lacuna Inc. by Dr Mierzwiak in the film *Eternal Sunshine of the Spotless Mind*, 2004). Thus, sometimes even a "weakening" can lead to improved behaviour or condition (Earp, Sandberg, Kahane, and Savulescu, 2014)..

4. Finally, performance can be improved by creating a capacity or disposition that is not present. This addition enables the subject to perform certain activities better and more efficiently. On the other hand, the definition refers only to the abilities already possessed by a subject.

These considerations evoke debates that have produced a vast philosophical literature. Our discussion points do not do justice to this complexity and richness. However, the only purpose for which they have been proposed is to highlight the difficulties raised by the initial definition. We will return to some of them when we consider the specific topic of this book, namely the acceptability of a particular form of enhancement, moral bioenhancement. We therefore propose to use the following definition of 'enhancement' in general, which is very similar to the one proposed by David DeGrazia (2014, p. 361):

> A deliberate intervention on a given subject that can employ various means and technologies to strengthen or reduce existing capabilities and desired characteristics or create new ones with the intention of improving their performance, activities, and condition of well-being.

According to this definition, biomedical technologies and more 'traditional' means can be considered enhancers, accepting at the descriptive level a continuity between methods in terms of enhancement effect. This does not mean that other considerations about their mode of action on individuals will lead to a more complex relationship between biomedical and non-biomedical means at the *regulatory level.* The definition also removes the reference to 'health' or 'normality' and thus the problematic distinction between therapies and enhancements, and includes the possibility of creating or reducing specific abilities.

The new definition retains the idea that enhancement aims to improve human form or function. However, it should be noted that the relationship between 'enhancement' and 'improvement' is complex, because not every enhancement is an improvement *tout court.* To enhance something is to amplify and increase it, to give more strength and significant development to the object you are working on. "Improving" implies a value judgement so that the result of the improvement action has produced, or is expected to produce, a higher result than the initial state. An improvement can have unexpected disastrous effects, even if it improves a particular performance. Consider, for example, an individual who has undergone a genetic modification during the embryonic phase that has resulted in an increase in height that is radically above average. In principle, this physical characteristic will allow them to reach heights that others cannot, giving them advantages in specific fields (for example, sport). However, such an increase may not be a real improvement, as excessive amplification of a trait may have a detrimental effect on the overall physical structure of the individual or become a lifelong handicap; i.e. if the height, instead of being an advantage, creates difficulties in adapting to the environment. As Bostrom and Sandberg point out, the human organism is a highly complex system:

> Evolution is a process powerful enough to have led to the development of systems— such as human brains—that are

> far more complex and capable than anything that human scientists or engineers have managed to design. Surely it would be foolish, absent supporting solid evidence, to suppose that we are currently likely to be able to do better than evolution, mainly when so far we have not even managed to understand the systems that evolution has designed and when our attempts even just to repair what evolution has built so often misfire! [...] The basic idea is simple. In order to decide whether we want to modify some aspect of a system, it is helpful to consider why the system has that aspect in the first place. Similarly, if we propose introducing a new feature, we might ask why the system does not already possess it. (Bostrom, Sandberg, 2009, p. 377)

Thus, although a specific capacity is enhanced in order to achieve an increase in value between the initial state (before the intervention) and the final state (after the intervention), it may be that, in some cases, an overall evaluation of the technique used leads to the conclusion that a given enhancement does not improve the overall state and is therefore undesirable or unacceptable. However, this moral and normative judgement is not about enhancement per se but some specific enhancement forms. As such, it is controversial and left to philosophical debate. Some enhancements may appear to be real improvements in theory but not in practice. When it is possible to implement a given technology, some observers may judge some enhancements as real improvements from their evaluative perspective. In contrast, other observers may make the opposite judgement.

In conclusion, the new definition may not be satisfactory to everyone and does not claim to be. However, we propose to use it in this book because we believe it captures the essential elements of the enhancement problem and can raise a sufficiently large number of ethical questions.

Moral (bio-)enhancement

This book is essentially concerned with a particular form of moral improvement, which at this point can be defined as follows:

> *Moral enhancement: a deliberate intervention on a given subject, using various means and technologies to strengthen or weaken existing capacities and dispositions, or to create new ones, with the intention of improving their moral motivation, decisions and behaviour.*

Traditional forms of moral reinforcement include all the well-known educational tools by which various figures attempt to change the dispositions and moral behavior of individuals: behavioural examples, explicit teaching, use of punishments, rewards, disincentives and incentives, blame and praise, and expressions of approval and disapproval. Personal critical reflection on one's own motives, beliefs and behaviour can also be seen as an improvement. However, the subject of this book is a specific form of moral enhancement that can be achieved through non-traditional interventions, namely moral bio-enhancement:

> *Moral bio-enhancement: a deliberate biomedical intervention on a given subject to enhance or reduce existing or create new abilities and dispositions to improve their moral motivation, decisions and behaviour.*

The means of moral bio-enhancement could include genetic engineering, replacing or correcting parts of the gene pool to restore desired sequences; pharmacological interventions; or neurological interventions (e.g. brain stimulation). The use of the conditional in this statement is necessary, however, because so far there is little evidence that biotechnology can actually influence morality. The experimental data often cited by proponents of moral bioenhancement are still controversial and seem to indicate that the road to safe and effective interventions is still long and full of obstacles (De Melo-Martín, Salles, 2015, pp. 229 -232; Wiseman, 2016, pp. 88-111; De Melo-Martín, 2018, pp. 27-33).

Let us now look at the most cited studies on pharmacological enhancement (Levy et al., 2014). Let us start with research on *implicit bias*, a term used in cognitive science to indicate a wide range of attitudes "acquired passively without individuals' awareness and that influence subsequent judgments, decisions, and actions without intention or volition. These subtle attitudes and beliefs have been variously labelled *implicit*, *unconscious*, or *automatic*." (Dasgupta, 2013, p. 235). Their unconscious and intuitive nature makes them difficult to 'penetrate' for introspection. It thus can guide reactions to certain groups of people without the subject being aware of it and in stark contrast to their explicit attitudes, beliefs, and convictions, which they accept as valid.

A common interpretation of implicit bias is that it involves unconscious evaluative judgments of various kinds, such as associations between gender and the ability to learn quickly, or succeed in science subjects (Axelson et al, 2010; Carlana, 2019), associations between skin colour and intellectual abilities and, in general, negative evaluative associations with people of colour (Amodio & Devine, 2006; Olson & Fazio, 2006); they can also generate various behaviours, ranging from an increase in blinking to the expression of signals of tension in the presence of members of certain groups, to different evaluative treatment in the school or work environment, up to severe reactions, such as greater ease in shooting at a person in response to perceived danger (Wood et al, 2009; Dovidio et al., 2002; Amodio, Harmon-Jones and Devine, 2003; Payne, 2005). Although empirical research has mainly focused on ethnic and gender bias, it is plausible to assume that implicit biases can also lead to discriminatory behaviour towards people with disabilities, the elderly, or members of the LGBTQ+ community. In general, actions influenced by implicit attitudes vary in their moral significance and may conflict with explicit attitudes. Even if people claim to have egalitarian and anti-discriminatory beliefs, convictions and value commitments, they may have implicit attitudes that are inconsistent with their explicit ones.

Implicit *biases* can be measured indirectly through a number of tests, the most famous of which is the IAT, the Implicit Association Test. This test consists of proposing some terms to the subject, who has to associate them with some categories or evaluative concepts as quickly as possible, making as few mistakes as possible. The experimenter then measures the subject's reaction time. The results show that people generally take longer and make more errors when it is possible to associate a particular term (e.g. a woman's name or skin colour) with stereotypical categories (e.g. family rather than career) or negative evaluative concepts (e.g. war). It is not entirely clear to what extent these tendencies manifest themselves in real life in relation to the laboratory and experimental measures offered in the literature, nor what their predictive power is in relation to subjects' behaviour. Further empirical evidence is needed to resolve such questions.

Philosophical reflection has shown an interest in the impact of implicit biases when they lead to morally unjust behaviour. For example, an implicit bias might lead an employer to recruit staff on the basis of gender or ethnicity, or a maths teacher to give different marks to female students even when they are equally deserving compared to their male peers. Regardless of the debate about the actual responsibility of the subject (Brownstein & Saul, 2016), the effects produced are undesirable and therefore it would be desirable to be able to correct the behaviour produced. According to some researchers, propranolol, an active beta-blocker commonly used to treat hypertension and various cardiovascular diseases, can significantly reduce implicit (but not explicit) racist bias: subjects who received the substance performed better on the IAT in terms of speed and consistency (Terbeck et al., 2012).

Other studies have explored the relationship between prosocial behaviour and serotonin, a neurotransmitter synthesised in the central nervous system that has multiple functions. Serotonin production promotes the control of violent impulses and reduces the emotions associated with responding to provocation (Krakowski, 2003; Crockett et al., 2010; Kuepper, 2010; Zak, 2012; Crockett et al., 2013). From some of this research, it appears that citalopram, belonging to the group of drugs called selective serotonin reuptake inhibitors (SSRIs), can make people "less likely to consider harm to one person morally acceptable in order to save many others" when they compare some hypothetical scenarios involving actions with these effects. In addition, people who play a particular activity called the "ultimatum game" also seem to benefit from the drug. In the basic version of the ultimatum game, two players, A and B, face each other: A offers B to share a certain amount of money. If B accepts, the sum is divided as proposed; if B refuses, neither player receives anything. In general, those who respond tend to punish bidders when the offer does not exceed 20-30% of the sum because it is judged unfair: "Rejecting unfair offers enforces a fairness norm but also harms the other player financially; responders are thus forced to tradeoff concerns for fairness versus harm when considering unfair offers." (Crockett et al., 2010, pp. 17434). After receiving citalopram, recipients were less likely to reduce the winnings of bidders who had offered unfair amounts. For this reason, the researchers interpreted the data as "evidence that serotonin enhances the aversiveness of harming others—either imagined harms (in the case of the hypothetical scenarios) or economic harms (in the case of the economic game)" (Crockett, 2014, p. 370).

Oxytocin also appears to have some behavioural effects. Called the "moral molecule" by some, its administration would affect trust and generosity (Zak et al, 2007; Hurleman et al, 2010; Zak, 2012). One study found that the substance made healthy male participants more likely to endorse choices that promoted selfish interests in the context of moral dilemmas. At the same time, the effect disappeared for choices that did not foresee such an outcome or that occurred in non-moral contexts. On the other hand, oxytocin produced different responses in healthy female participants, who were more likely to express altruistic preferences in the same moral dilemmas. As the researchers conclude, the data suggest a "dimorphism in human moral behaviour" that has evolutionary roots in the protection and care of offspring (Scheele et al., 2014). Beyond this explanation, other studies suggest that oxytocin can also have immoral effects. For example, Shalvi and De Dreu (2014) found that some subjects receiving oxytocin lied more often and more quickly to benefit members of their group than subjects receiving placebo, even when there was no expectation that other members would reciprocate in the future. In addition, some genetic variants appear to influence the moral judgement of actions that inadvertently cause harm. Subjects who carry them appear to judge this behaviour significantly more negatively than those who do not (Walter et al., 2012).

Non-pharmacological interventions have also been tested. Several studies have subjected some people to transcranial magnetic stimulation. This technique uses electrical pulses to create an electromagnetic field that penetrates the skull and stimulates nerve tissue or transcranial direct current stimulation (tDCS), which stimulates the brain with low-intensity direct currents. The use of these devices in specific brain areas can alter moral judgement, decision-making in solving moral dilemmas, and pro-social behaviour (i.e., altruism, trust, cooperation) (Darby & Pascual-Leone, 2017). Given the complex relationship between genes and the environment, the possibility of intervening at the genetic level to enhance morality is pure speculation. However, it has been suggested that in the future it might be possible to use gene editing techniques to make biological changes to those parts of the genome associated with virtuous or violent and antisocial behaviour, or to select embryos that promise to be carriers of such genetic variants (Douglas, 2008, p. 233; Faust, 2008;

Walker, 2009; Zarpentine, 2013, pp. 145-147). Finally, we can think of forms of moral enhancement that do not directly intervene in the biological nature of human beings, but use other technological means, such as robotics, artificial intelligence and virtual reality (Savulescu & Maslen, 2015; Borenstein & Arkin, 2016; Giubilini & Savulescu, 2018; Rueda & Lara, 2020; Lara, 2021).

Why Do We Need Moral Bio-enhancement?

Julian Savulescu and Ingmar Persson, who have dedicated several essays to this topic, are certainly among the first authors to propose and defend the necessity of moral bio-enhancement. However, it is in Unfit for the Future (2012) that the two philosophers provide the full picture into which their idea of moral bio-enhancement fits. In this book, Savulescu and Persson outline the current state of human life on the planet, characterised by current and potential threats to the survival of large parts of the world's population. The macro-problem facing humanity is technological development, which, together with certain beneficial outcomes, exponentially increases the capacity for destruction: "It is plausible that within a decade or so, the advancement of scientific technology will allow a single person, adequately trained, to destroy all higher forms of life on Earth" (Persson & Savulescu, 2019a, p. 66). Terrorist groups could acquire devastating nuclear and biological weapons, which would trigger revenge and retaliation motivated by fear and xenophobia. This "destructive escalation" could be facilitated by the development of cognitive biomedical enhancements capable of improving memory, self-control, attention and alertness, and thus accelerating the acquisition of knowledge. According to Persson and Savulescu:

> [the] expansion of scientific knowledge and cognitive ability will put in an increasing number of people's hands 'weapons of mass destruction' or the ability to deploy them. In so far as this is so, this growth of knowledge will be instrumentally bad for us on the whole, by unacceptably increasing the risk that we shall die soon. It will be bad for us that scientific knowledge continues to grow by traditional means, and even worse if this growth is further accelerated by biomedical or

> genetic enhancement of our cognitive capacities (Savulescu and Persson, 2008, p. 166).

Western societies also suffer from the "tragedy of the commons". Their populations have become so large that the sum of their citizens' actions can cause significant damage to the climate and the environment, even if each individual action has a negligible impact. What is needed, therefore, is strong internal cooperation among the richest countries and, at the same time, a foreign policy that coordinates the efforts of each rich country (ibid., pp. 94 and 104). The only viable solutions involve a fundamental transformation of our liberal democracies. According to Persson and Savulescu, the possibility of countering the evil uses of technology will depend on a policy of substantial restrictions on privacy: surveillance of public and private spaces could be the key to preventing terrorist attacks. All the precautions taken could harden to the point of becoming unsustainable and motivate discriminatory policies against some ethnic groups to which the terrorists belong. According to the authors, such restrictions would be justified by even the minimal probability of such massive damage occurring. Similarly, climate and environmental change can only be tackled through restrictive policies that limit citizens' lifestyles, consumption, behaviour and the production systems of the richest and most polluting countries. There are political and economic problems in enforcing such choices, both domestically and internationally, as individual and collective self-interests could (and already do) delay the necessary global changes.

In general, Persson and Savulescu are sceptical about the ability of liberal democracies to adequately address the macro problems that characterise Extreme Damage, i.e. the potential annihilation of all forms of life worth living on Earth due to technological development and environmental degradation. This scepticism is fundamentally motivated by the fact that both citizens and rulers are affected by psychological limitations that prevent them from making the right decisions in many cases. Common-sense morality, that is, the "set of moral attitudes that act as a common denominator of differently specified morals in human societies around the world" (Persson & Savulescu, 2019a, p. 27), has the following characteristics:

a. Believes that everyone should be protected from interference by others (negative rights doctrine). The emphasis on the right not to be interfered with in our activities derives from the fact that it is much more difficult to do harm to an organism than to do good to it. To harm an organism, it is enough to remove one of the many conditions that allow it to remain healthy and alive. To benefit, we must understand the condition for which its function is improved. Furthermore, we can easily cause many deaths and injuries (for example, by driving a car at an insane speed into a crowd of people). However, we have fewer opportunities to save the same number of lives and prevent the same amount of damage (ibid, pp. 28-39).

b. It involves a conception of responsibility on a causal basis, whereby we are more responsible for the events we produce or cause than for the events we allow to happen. Causal responsibility is also diluted when we contribute to events whose production depends on the action of several agents. Suppose a hundred people walking along a pavement each kick a fence, with the ultimate effect of destroying it. The causal contribution of each of them to the destruction of the fence will be less than the accidental contribution of one person destroying the fence alone. Moreover, the responsibility will also be judged to be less (ibid, pp. 39-43).

c. A *bias towards the near future* characterises it. We tend to feel "relieved if something unpleasant that was supposed to happen to us in the near future is postponed; instead, we feel disappointment if something pleasant is postponed that was in store for us in the near future, where the same postponement of unpleasant and pleasant things in a more distant future would have left us indifferent" (ibid, p. 44). There is no such bias for space; we care about our pain and suffering and that of our acquaintances regardless of the distance we or our acquaintances are from the present place. However, we would be more concerned about a stranger suffering close to us than a stranger suffering many miles away. The activation of sympathetic concern when strangers are involved thus depends on spatial proximity, and, unlike temporal bias, spatial bias does not lead us to ignore the importance of well-being by increasing the distance from those who suffer at the cost of suffering more, just as we postpone our suffering into the future at the cost of making it worse (ibid, p. 47).

d. Our capacity for sympathetic and altruistic concern is also limited by the fact that we do not know how to respond in a morally adequate way when a large number of subjects are involved. The more people we have to sympathise with, the more our capacity for sympathetic moral response and the amount of help we are willing to give to each of them is reduced. Similarly, our synchronic cooperation skills weaken when we have to cooperate with more people or over a longer period of time. In these cases, the ability to accurately identify who is deflecting or opportunistically taking advantage of cooperation is lost. Selflessness and trust are attitudes that are strengthened in smaller groups or communities but tend to fade as numbers increase. We become more suspicious of strangers, which explains the spread of xenophobic attitudes in humanity (ibid., pp. 55-56).
e. Human beings are capable of moral emotions associated with altruism and a sense of justice (gratitude, anger, guilt, shame, remorse, forgiveness, etc.), i.e. of sympathising with the suffering of others and of reciprocating the benefits and harms received, but, in the light of the previous points, there are many limits to the manifestation of these emotions, linked to the nature and number of recipients, to temporal and spatial distances, to the causal genesis of the damage that occurs (ibid., pp. 48-55).

According to Persson and Savulescu, common sense morality is the evolutionary product of the natural history of human beings, and its structure depends on the adaptive advantages it has brought to humanity over many millennia. In the face of the extraordinary problems of today's world, the psychological dispositions that characterise the morality of common sense are wholly inadequate. They have been consolidated in such a way that small and highly homogeneous groups within them can face up to environmental challenges that involve, above all, the possibility of inflicting and receiving personal harm that manifests itself in the immediate present. Within these communities, it was possible to develop bonds of trust and cooperation because the subjects willing to cooperate were easily identifiable, and the boundaries separating members of one's own social group from strangers were clear and roughly coincided with those of the community. As Persson and Savulescu point out

> Scientific and technological progress have radically changed the conditions of human life. Through virtually all of their history, humans have lived in societies small enough for everybody to know each other, with simple technology which permitted them to affect only their immediate surroundings, and only in the immediate future. But today, humans live in huge societies with an advanced technology which enables them to affect the environment globally, far into the future. We hypothesized, based on evidence from evolutionary biology and psychology, that the moral psychology of humans is adapted to the former conditions, which have obtained for most of the time the human species has existed. This mismatch is a serious matter because humans now have at their disposal technology so powerful that it could bring about the destruction of technology so powerful at their disposal that it could destroy the whole planet if misused. (Persson and Savulescu, 2013, p. 124)

Liberal democracies and their citizens find themselves unable to make the appropriate choices to counter the prospect of extreme damage, the disappearance of all life worth living on Earth. Individual and collective education, socialisation, reflection and imagination are the methods on which humanity has traditionally relied to solve problems. However, they do not seem to be fast enough to keep up with technological development and are therefore unlikely to be sufficient to cope with crises (Persson & Savulescu, 2019a, p. 128). The only way out, according to the authors, is large-scale moral bio-enhancement, which allows for the intensification of "the will of the population to act morally" (ibid., p. 126), and this is only possible at the cost of overcoming the intrinsic limits of common sense morality as it has been outlined. Strictly speaking, moral bio-enhancement must aim to strengthen moral dispositions such as *altruism*, the ability to empathise with the suffering of others and to act accordingly to eliminate it, and *justice*, the ability to respond with gratitude and reciprocity to those who do us good and with anger and vengeance to those who do us harm. In a broader sense, it must instead aim to correct the bias towards the near future and the causal conception of responsibility. Persson and Savulescu are confident that biomedical interventions to achieve this will be available in the future, as ethnological, psychological, neuroscientific and evolutionary studies have amply demonstrated the biological nature of these provisions.

Persson and Savulescu argue that the limits of common sense morality lead to the search for effective forms of moral bio-enhancement that allow the prevention of extreme harm. Other proponents of moral bio-enhancement interpret the limits of human nature differently, proposing justifications for moral bio-enhancement that are closer to the motivations that lead to the development of the Ludovico technique in *A Clockwork Orange*: human nature is inherently flawed because it contains evil tendencies that explain the flourishing of violence, assault, rape, etc. If this anthropological premise is accepted, the prospects for moral bio-enhancement are limited. If this anthropological premise is accepted, the prospects of radically eliminating evil by relying on traditional means such as socialisation and education are bound to be disillusioning. What is needed is a change in human *biological* nature, given the considerable evidence that, for example, there are links between behaviour and our genetic heritage (Walker, 2009, pp. 27-29; DeGrazia, 2014, p. 362). Alternatively, the acceptability of the perspective of people who will be able to enhance themselves morally is independent of the existence of objective conditions that require it. Unlike other enhancement interventions, it does not create inequalities. One of the most common objections to cognitive or physical enhancement is precisely the effect that such interventions have on equality of opportunity. A person whose intelligence, memory, muscles and stature have been enhanced by biomedical means acquires an unfair advantage that sharpens the logic of competition in certain fields (education, science, work), while other values should be privileged. However controversial these arguments may be, moral bio-enhancement does not seem to have this effect. The presence in future societies of individuals with more moral reasoning, thanks to genetic or pharmacological interventions, will only benefit the rest of the population (for a different assessment from an egalitarian perspective, see Sparrow, 2014b). The most robust justification for the introduction of moral bio-enhancement then lies in the weakness of the objections to enhancement raised by bio-conservative positions (Douglas, 2008, pp. 229-230). Whatever the motivation, the project of moral bioenhancement of humanity seems as fascinating as it is controversial (Hauskeller & Coyne, 2018; Lavazza & Reichlin, 2019a). We can now move on to assess the more problematic implications of this proposal.

CHAPTER 2

What Does Moral Bio-enhancement Augment?

What Morality are We Speaking Of?

In the first chapter, we focused on the meaning and types of 'enhancement' and the reasons that have led some authors to defend the introduction of moral 'bio-enhancement'. In this chapter, however, we will focus on the meaning of 'morality'.

In the field of ethics, there are different ways of understanding this term and it is therefore necessary to have a map, albeit a very simplified one, of the main ethical theories that could be relevant to the topic we are dealing with. Indeed, it can be argued that our moral judgements are the product of our emotional life ("moral sentimentality") or of our reason ("moral rationalism"). Furthermore, we may think that an action is moral or immoral because of the consequences it produces, because it follows or does not follow certain principles, or because it derives from certain character traits, called virtues and vices. These are familiar distinctions to those who study moral philosophy, and they are necessary to understand what we need to strengthen

To understand the alternative between sentimentality and rationalism in ethics, we will refer to the philosophy of David Hume (1711-1776) and that of Immanuel Kant (1724-1804), respectively, and give only some basic information about these two approaches.

According to David Hume, philosophy and common sense are based on the idea that there is an eternal conflict between passion and reason, and that virtue consists in the triumph of reason: "Every rational creature is bound to regulate his actions according to the dictates of reason" and to reconcile any motive or principle that is contrary to the canon of reason (Hume, 1971b, pp. 433-434). Hume proposes instead to overturn this consolidated pattern by recognising that reason cannot determine our will, although it helps us to understand reality better. When reason deals with appearances, it abstracts from the world of real things to which will belongs. In other situations, however, it makes us see the relationship between objects, and this function is beneficial. If we anticipate that an object will cause pleasure or pain, we feel an inclination or aversion to it and regulate our actions accordingly. If we recognise that the object has certain relationships with other objects, we can extend these emotions to those other objects. The passions are not aroused by reason, although it can guide them. Reason is inert, as it cannot generate actions or desires, nor can it suppress a desire or passion. Sometimes we feel certain emotions, such as fear and joy, which seem to be modifiable by reason. For example, we may be afraid of a dark cave because we think it hides some danger or threat. In this case, our emotion is accompanied by a judgement or opinion that can be corrected by reason, i.e. if we understand that there is nothing to fear, our fear may disappear or change. This is a phenomenon of which Hume is well aware. What he excludes is that reason can justify our value judgments that arise from our passions and desires: in fact, in a famous passage, he argues that, from the point of view of reason, there is nothing wrong with preferring the destruction of the world to a scratch on the fingers, nor with choosing one's own ruin in order to spare a little pain to a completely unknown person:

> It is as little contrary to reason to prefer even my own acknowledged lesser good to my greater, and have a more ardent affection for the former than the latter. A trivial good may, from certain circumstances, produce a desire superior to what arises from the greatest and most valuable enjoyment; nor is there anything more extraordinary in this, than in mechanics to see one pound weight raise up a hundred by the advantage of its situation. (ibid, p. 437).

In short, reason fails to motivate actions nor justify our assessments. The emphasis placed on the powers of reason both by philosophy and by common sense derives, according to Hume, from the need to explain the existence of many discussions, not only philosophical, such as those on moral questions (Hume, 1971a, p. 181), and from the fact that sometimes " calm desires and tendencies, which, though they are real passions, produce little emotion in mind, and are more known by their effects than by the immediate feeling or sensation"(Hume, 1971b, p. 438). In these cases, natural instincts such as benevolence and resentment, tenderness towards children, or the general desire for good and general aversion to evil considered in themselves (i.e., without references to specific objects) can be mistaken for determinations of reason.

This general scheme also applies to the moral sphere. Hume notes that if morality is to be truly practical, that is, to influence human action, it must maintain a connection with the motives of the will. If morality is a phenomenon that "excites passions, and produces or prevents actions", then "the rules of morality are not the conclusions of our reason" (ibid., p. 483). Therefore, the merit or demerit of actions does not stem from their adherence to rational standards, but rather from other sources. Reason is not the source of moral good and evil, nor the origin of the moral distinctions we use to judge behaviour. Even in the moral sphere, reason retains its function as a "guide", revealing the existence of objects and properties, and discovering the causal connections and relationships between means and ends (ibid., pp. 485-487). Even if we could identify eternal laws that impose obligations on every rational being, we would then have to demonstrate the necessary connection between the relations on which these laws are based and the will. But this connection is impossible to establish because of the inertia of reason: "It is one thing to know virtue, and quite another to conform the will to it" (ibid., p. 492).

According to Hume, moral distinctions are not the product of reason, nor are they relations known to reason. First, morality does not consist of principles and relations that reason can discover and impose on all rational beings, regardless of their experience and concrete life. When such relations arise, a particular moral judgement should automatically follow, but this is not the case. Let us take the case of incest, a practice that is judged so differently depending on whether it occurs between animals or between human beings: an innocent act in the first case, a shameful act in the second. Why this difference in judgement? Perhaps because human beings have a reason capable of detecting the shamefulness of this behaviour, which other animals do not have?

According to Hume, this answer would demonstrate that "every animal that possesses sense, appetites and will, that is to say, all animals, must be capable of all the same virtues and vices based on which we praise and blame human creatures. The only difference is that the superiority of our reason can serve to discover vice or virtue, and in this way it can increase blame or praise" (ibid., p. 495). These distinctions are independent of reason and created by the will and appetites. The only difference would be that human beings, unlike other animals, are aware of them.

Furthermore, it is questionable whether ethics is a form of knowledge of objective moral properties. Let us take a premeditated crime, says Hume, and break it down, analyse it, and divide it in search of that component which we call "vice". We will never find it, but we will find "certain passions, motives, wills, and thoughts" (ibid., p. 496). For Hume, vice and virtue are analogous to properties such as sounds, colours, heat and cold, which are not objective qualities but subjective perceptions. The sentimental nature of virtue and vice is evidenced by the pleasant character of the former and the unpleasant character of the latter. Noble and generous actions are lovable, while ignoble and unjust actions arouse aversion:

> To have a sense of virtue, is nothing but to feel a satisfaction of a particular kind from the contemplation of a character. The very feeling constitutes our praise or admiration. We go no farther; nor do we enquire into the cause of the satisfaction. We do not infer a character to be virtuous, because it pleases: But in feeling that it pleases after such a particular manner, we in effect feel that it is virtuous. (Ibid, p. 497).

The pleasure associated with virtue, however, has a peculiar character. It is not the same feeling we get when we drink good wine or listen to good music. We can only speak of moral feeling when we are looking at a particular character in general, and not at ourselves. The moral perspective therefore transcends the interests of the judge. Moreover, character traits are associated with love and hate, pride and humility, a relationship that does not exist when dealing with inanimate objects (ibid., pp. 499-500). Feelings of approval and disgust are natural, both in the sense of not being miraculous and in the sense of being frequent.

According to Hume, they are phenomena so ingrained in our constitution that it is impossible to eliminate them without at the same time disturbing the human mind.

For Hume, therefore, moral judgments are nothing more than linguistic formulations of feelings of approval or disapproval, and have as their object not actions in and of themselves, but the character of men, that set of qualities which tend to benefit themselves and others (virtues), and qualities which tend instead to harm themselves and others (vices). Hume is convinced that "actions, in themselves, if they do not derive from a constant principle, have no influence on love or hatred, pride or humility, and consequently are never considered in morals". Actions are virtuous or vicious in so far as they depend on a character, that is, on "permanent principles of the mind, which extend to all conduct" (ibid., p. 608).

Several principles govern the relationship between character and valuation, and Hume analyses them carefully. A central role is given to the "principle of sympathy". For Hume, sympathy is not a fundamental moral disposition, but a mechanism that allows the sharing of feelings and passions among human beings and therefore dramatically influences moral judgements (ibid., pp. 332-334 and 609-611). Nevertheless, sympathy has limits dictated by proximity. The further one is from other people in space and time, the more difficult it is to empathise with their passions, feelings, sufferings, joys, approvals and disapprovals. Moral judgments can have coherence and stability only when "we fix certain firm and general points of view, and always, in our thoughts, we refer to them, whatever our current situation" (ibid, p. 615). The achievement of such a point of view is possible thanks to experience and imagination: if we compare the reliable and loyal character of a person close to us with that of Socrates, as Plato presents him in the Crito, we can undoubtedly sympathise with him more easily, but we do not claim that he is more praiseworthy than the Athenian philosopher. This is because "we know that if we were as close to [Socrates], he would inspire us with a much greater sense of affection and admiration" (ibid.). Thanks to the imaginative effort that brings us close to Socrates, we can correct our judgments of blame and praise.

Therefore, according to Hume, reason assists in identifying the most appropriate means when it comes to choosing and acting. However, it is the passions and desires that determine the ends and move us to action;

stable and enduring, capable of benefiting or harming ourselves and/or others (virtues and vices), the more we arouse approval or disapproval in others. Morality is therefore explained on an essentially sentimental basis.

On the other hand, the moral philosophy of Immanuel Kant is profoundly opposed, according to which the central concept of ethics is that of "good will", which, though not the only good, is the "highest good" (Kant, 1995b, p. 52). For Kant, morality does not depend on the moral quality of the effects we can produce in the world, nor on our ability to achieve the goals we set for ourselves. We behave morally only when our will is motivated by the idea of "duty". Whereas Hume admits that the morally good will is moved by a plurality of desires, inclinations, and qualities, Kant recognises a single moral principle and rules out the possibility that a person driven to act by an inclination is truly acting morally. Although acts done out of interest or profit are indistinguishable from those done out of duty, it is possible to distinguish between principles. Morally speaking, a merchant who acts honestly because he feels it is his duty to do so out of respect for his customers is different from a merchant who does not deceive his customers in order not to ruin his business. All actions motivated by "immediate inclination", natural and spontaneous impulses, such as the instinct to preserve one's life or natural sympathy, are apparently in accordance with duty, but are not performed for duty. Kant writes in *The Groundwork of the Metaphysics of Morals*:

To be beneficent where one can is a duty, and besides this, there are some souls so sympathetically attuned that, even without any other motive of vanity or utility to self, take an inner gratification in spreading joy around them, and can take delight in the contentment of others insofar as it is their own work. But I assert that in such a case the action, however it may conform to duty and however amiable it is, nevertheless has no true moral worth, but is on the same footing as other inclinations, e.g., the inclination to honor, which, when it fortunately encounters something that in fact serves the common good and is in conformity with duty, and is thus worthy of honor, deserves praise and encouragement, but not esteem; for the maxim lacks moral content, namely of doing such actions not from inclination but from duty. (Ibid, p. 54).

Furthermore, in the *Critique of Practical Reason*, he reiterates that, while he appreciates beneficent acts motivated by love or benevolence, they are to be regarded as alien to morality in the strict sense:

> It is a very beautiful thing to do good to men from love to them and from sympathetic good will, or to be just from love of order; but this is not yet the true moral maxim of our conduct which is suitable to our position amongst rational beings as men, when we pretend with fanciful pride to set ourselves above the thought of duty, like volunteers, and, as if we were independent on the command, to want to do of our own good pleasure what we think we need no command to do. (Kant 1995a, p. 225)

For Kant, sympathy, the participation in the suffering of others that leads us to act altruistically, is a "pathological motive" because it excludes the effort required in choosing to obey the moral law, which requires the will (ibid., pp. 227-228).

This is a very different approach from Hume, not only because of the contemptuous judgement reserved for sympathy, but also because the true moral maxim of behaviour must conform to the rational nature of man. This conformity is measured neither by the end to which the action is directed, nor by the (beneficial) consequences that the action produces, but is given by the principle that inspires the particular action. If this principle can be desired to become a universal law acceptable to all rational beings, then we are faced with a genuine moral motive. The most famous example is the false promise: is it lawful to promise something knowing that you cannot keep it in a given situation? According to Kant, if we tried to universalise this maxim (promise even if you know you cannot keep your word) until it becomes a law that commands you to lie, a contradiction would arise: "once this law is established, there would no longer be any promise, it would be useless to declare my will concerning future actions because the others would not believe my declarations or, if they did it recklessly, they would repay me with equal money, with the consequence that my maxim, once transformed into a universal law, could not to avoid destroying oneself "(ibid., p. 59).

The moral law therefore has an absolute necessity for all rational beings: moral principles have the form of categorical imperatives (you must), which unconditionally bind the conduct of human beings, who are always tempted to take interests and desires as motives for their actions, inclinations, etc. They are not hypothetical imperatives, which command an action only insofar as it is necessary to satisfy a desire (if you want to get rich, save). They are not, therefore, hypothetical imperatives, which command an action only in so far as it is necessary to satisfy the desire (if you want to get rich, save). The typical categorical imperative formula is presented in the Critique of Practical Reason: "act so that the maxim of thy will can always at the same time hold good as a principle of universal legislation." (Kant, 1995a, p. 167). Moreover, for Kant, human beings do not know this fundamental law of practical reason from experience, but are immediately aware of it as a "fact of reason" (ibid., p. 168).

Authentic good will is not motivated by inclinations, desires, and interests, but is determined autonomously from them only by conformity to the representation of duty. Kantian ethics is primarily a formal ethics, that is, it aims to establish some procedural characteristics of morality (necessity, universality, rationality). But there is also a substantive side to the categorical imperative. The rational nature of human beings is fundamental to establishing the form of moral law. However, Kant recognises that it has an absolute value, so much so that: "man and, in general, every reasonable being, exists as an end in itself, not simply as a means to be used by this or that will: but in all its actions, both those that concern it on its own and those that concern other reasonable beings, it must always be considered at the same time as an end" (Kant 1995b, p. 86). When we ask ourselves what to do and weigh up the various options available to us, our decision is constrained both by the formal representation of the will, by the universalisation of our maxim, and by the recognition of the nature of an end in itself or, as Kant puts it, by the intrinsic dignity of both our person and the person of others. This dimension of dignity does not allow one to use one's own person and the person of others as mere tools to achieve certain ends. The recognition of this value, however, is only possible thanks to reason.

Hume and Kant represent the two paradigmatic poles of the confrontation in ethics, with Aristotle (384/383 B.C. - 322 B.C.) in the middle. Like Hume, Aristotle believes that the central element of ethics is not duty, but the character of the human being, made up of virtues and vices. Unlike Hume, however, he argued that virtue is primarily a habitual disposition to make choices that identify a happy medium between two vicious extremes (one for excess and one for defect), and he held that reason has no subsidiary role with respect to the passions. The moral virtues exercise their dominion over the passions and desires that are capable of "following the rule", that is, of being formed by the rational part of the soul and, more precisely, by wisdom, defined as "a truthful habitual state, coupled with practical reasoning, concerning what is good and evil for man" (Aristotle, 1999, p. 231). Wisdom is an "intellectual virtue", a disposition of the rational part of the soul that performs the function of guiding action through deliberation. The wise, therefore, are those who know how to deliberate well about good and evil for human beings (ibid., p. 237). Good deliberation is that which not only makes it clear what is right, but also because it is right in view of the end of the "good life in general" (ibid., p. 231).

Moreover, the good life, which we might also call the happy life, consists precisely in living according to virtue (ibid., pp. 21-22). From these few lines we can see that Aristotle does not devalue the passionate and desirous side of human nature, but believes that it can never lead to the good if it is not dominated and guided by reason. Therefore, it is not possible to correctly identify and practise virtue in the various areas in which it manifests itself unless the individual is first educated and then accustomed to acting generously, reasonably, courageously, etc., so that he acquires the ability to form his own will and to moderate his passions in the service of the true good and not of apparent goods (ibid., pp. 57-65).

In the end, then, this brief review gives us three different conceptions of ethics: the first, which goes back to Hume, for whom feelings and passions are the origin of judgement and moral behaviour; the second, which goes back to Kant, for whom reason is the epicentre of all judgement and action in the moral field; the third, which goes back to Aristotle, for whom it is instead practical wisdom that allows us to recognise and practise virtue and the good life.

A further complication is that sentimentalism and rationalism, in addition to trying to provide a convincing account of moral psychology, are also trying to answer some questions that belong in the realm of metaethics. That is, they concern the questions that can be raised about the nature of moral judgments, whether they are expressions of moral feelings of approval or disapproval, or judgments that capture moral truths and/or moral principles independent of experience. Sentimentality and rationalism can then be combined in different ways with normative theories that establish the criteria for judging a particular action to be good or bad, or right or wrong, and for deciding what to do in problematic cases. In philosophy, rationalism can be combined with both a theory of duty, such as Kantian deontology, and a theory of consequences, such as utilitarianism. In utilitarianism, the reasoning to be applied is identified with a calculation of the utility (in terms of pleasure, satisfaction of preferences, happiness, etc.) that each action can produce for the greatest number of people. Thus, in order to know whether a given action already performed is good or bad, it is necessary to determine whether it has produced consequences that maximise utility better than other actions that could have been performed. When we have to choose what to do in a given situation, we have to anticipate and calculate the utility produced by the actions we can perform. Furthermore, as we have seen, the ethics of virtue can have both a sentimentalist (Hume) and a rationalist (Aristotle) character.

The Moral Brain

An update of the debate on ethics comes from the cognitive sciences, which have conducted numerous types of research to understand the biological basis of moral judgement and action and their actual nature (Corbellini and Sirgiovanni, 2013, chap. 5; Christensen et al., 2014; Galletti, 2011; Songhorian, 2020). The large amount of data accumulated in many studies suggests a rather complex picture of the neuroscientific and genetic roots of morality.

According to Joshua Greene, for example, our brains operate in a dual mode. When it comes to making moral judgments about "impersonal" dilemmas, that is, dilemmas that imply a certain distance between those who have to make the decision and those who will suffer the consequences, the area of the brain corresponding to the dorsolateral prefrontal cortex, which is mainly delegated to cognitive control, is activated. Imagine this scene: An out-of-control train is speeding towards a group of workers on the tracks. You cannot warn them of the impending danger, but you can pull a lever to divert it to a siding where only one worker is present. In this case, those called upon to respond to the moral dilemma are likely to reflect for a long time on the possible solution, and ultimately choose to pull the lever and save the greatest number of lives. In 'personal' dilemmas, where there is no distance, the medial prefrontal cortex, some areas of the ventromedial prefrontal cortex and the amygdala are more activated. In fact, all of these areas play an important role in emotional processes. Let's modify the previous scene: this time you are on a bridge above the tracks, together with an obese person. The only way to stop the crazy train is to push this person onto the tracks, ensuring his death but preventing the vehicle from killing the five workers. As in the previous scene, it is a question of causing one death to save five lives, but the "personal" contact that the solution to the dilemma implies determines the activation of different brain processes. Faced with this version of the dilemma, subjects will mostly be reluctant to consider the sacrifice of the person as morally right and will immediately refuse to choose this option (Edmonds, 2014).

Greene's explanatory theory rests on two premises. The first suggests that mechanisms implemented in the way the human brain (our neural architecture) exists cause us to decide and act in a certain way without being able to consciously perceive the reasons for those decisions and actions. Psychological automatism also applies to the moral sphere, so that we have strong intuitions that guide us in our behaviour, but which we cannot justify. The answers we sometimes try to give to these moral reactions, for example in the face of the condemnation of incest, are merely "confabulations" (Haidt, 2001).

The other premise concerns the distinction between deontology and consequentialism. According to Greene, so-called ethical theories are not "philosophical inventions" but "natural psychological genres". Moral theories would therefore not be buildings erected by philosophers starting from nothing, but manifestations of different psychological models (Greene, 2007, p. 37). Moral theories are then the tips of icebergs submerged in the sea of neural connections, and it is for this reason that Greene uses these terms in a non-technical sense. Greene therefore distinguishes between 'characteristically consequentialist conclusions', which take the consequences produced as central to the decision about what to do, and 'characteristically deontological conclusions', which appeal instead to a priori moral principles (ibid., pp. 38-39). If deontological conclusions are motivated by emotions, then deontology in the broad sense is also driven by emotions. Rationalist deontology, such as Kant's, would then be a simple a posteriori rationalisation (or confabulation) of moral intuitions that precede reflective consciousness.

The division of 'mental work' assigns to personal dilemmas intuitive and emotional responses of a deontological nature, because they reflect an immediate reaction to actions that do not depend on any evaluation of their consequences. Impersonal dilemmas, on the other hand, receive consequentialist, reflexive and cognitive responses, and generally take longer to elaborate because they must impose themselves on what would otherwise be our immediate reactions. This subdivision determines what Greene calls the "dual process" of moral psychology, in which the most thoughtful responses, which involve the application of rules, struggle against immediate and intuitive responses. The psychological genres of ethical theory are, therefore, divided between cognition (utilitarianism) and emotion (deontology). In the case of personal dilemmas, the emotional response is so strong that reason is only able to overcome it in a minority of cases. Our reaction is so visceral and powerful that utilitarian reasoning can hardly set it aside and guide the choice.

For Greene, the dual structure of our psychology can be explained in evolutionary terms. Cooperation between groups is favoured by some automatic tendencies at the emotional level, which also explain the immediate response that the subjects tend to give to the dilemma above. The human brain is structured like a digital camera, in which the automatic settings and the manual mode together contribute to a better result because each pursues different "values": efficiency for the former and flexibility for the latter. This architecture provides the resources needed to manage conflicts and respond to dilemmas. Consequentialism and deontology are therefore not rival theories, but psychological genres that share the "mental work" and potentially allow us to find stability in our moral responses.

To complete the picture, it is necessary to mention some works that instead support the plausibility of a virtues approach to moral questions, suggested by the study of the functioning of some brain areas. William Casebeer and Patricia Churchland have argued that neuroscience describes the functioning of moral judgement and choice in a way similar to an Aristotelian conception of ethics. In the Aristotelian model, the virtuous sage can grasp the morally salient aspects of the situation and respond with good deliberation and the right passions; neuroscience suggests that moral cognition consists of the appropriate coordination of stimuli and executions, desires and affections (Casebeer & Churchland, 2003; Casebeer, 2005).

Other authors have suggested that the clues provided by empirical data can be taken into account without abandoning the space of 'reflexivity' that should characterise moral experience. We have already seen how Kant and Aristotle respectively assigned a reflective role to universalisation and practical deliberation. But Hume also asserted the need to take a firm and general standpoint in order to correct and stabilise one's moral judgements. From this point of view, and with a certain originality, Hanno Sauer proposed to attribute an emotional nature to our moral intuitions, without considering them impenetrable to cognitive analysis. The process of continuous revision and refinement of our intuitions and judgments is distributed over time and space: first, it takes place by comparing the responses we give in a diachronic sense to the moral challenges that lie ahead; second, it implies an intersubjective comparison that leads to an improvement in the interaction between intuitive and controlled cognition (Sauer, 2017). Sarah Songhorian, on the other hand, defended a model that takes up the reflective sentimentality of Adam Smith, in whose work we can find valuable information to better understand the relationship between reason and sentiment in ethics. According to Smith, sympathy and imagination play an important role in ethics. Sympathy allows us to share feelings. Imagination allows us to put ourselves in the shoes of others in order to judge the extent to which their passions match our own, and thus determine whether or not we can approve of them. Imagination also allows us to introject the gaze of others in order to judge our own emotions. These mental operations, however, are always subject to the influences of the culture in which one grows up and to the various distortions of individual judgement; the possibility of overcoming these limits and errors is entrusted to the "impartial spectator", to one:

> figure of moral conscience, which is not only the internalisation of real spectators with all their limitations but allows the subject to reach a higher level of moral judgment, a level that allows a critique of the moral rules of the society in which he lives and which it is not limited to contingency. [...] The impartial spectator [...] aspires to consider all

> possible perspectives, even simply imaginable, to arrive at the judgment worthy of approval. (Songhorian, 2020, p. 50).

The impartial spectator is a rational construction that represents the reflective capacity of the human being. According to Songhorian, the impartial spectator intervenes when the situation in front of us is unprecedented compared to those already experienced, and therefore cannot be dealt with by recourse to the rules and automatic behaviours formed thanks to past experience. The Smithian model is compatible with empirical data because it can explain both the role of emotion and that of reason in morality (ibid., pp. 112-120).

What Should We Enhance? Sentiments or Reason?

The availability of philosophical and scientific theories on the nature of morality is remarkable. It therefore seems particularly complex to understand what the goal of moral bio-enhancement should be. As we have seen, the map of interpretations of the moral phenomenon is particularly complex: to obtain moral bioenhancement, do we have to act on virtues, sympathetic dispositions, and reason? And which kind? And what kind of reason? The one that calculates the utility produced by alternative actions, the one that universalises the norms and reasons that one wants to adopt in order to act, or the practical reasoning that is part of the model of virtues? Persson and Savulescu are convinced that sympathetic altruism and a sense of justice are part of the core of morality, both because they have a biological basis and do not depend on cultural variations, and because there is a broad consensus around them regardless of which ethical theory is accepted (Persson & Savulescu, 2018, p. 168). Douglas argues that negative interventions should be preferred, at least those aimed at mitigating "anti-moral emotions" that interfere with moral motives. These include "strong aversion to certain racial groups" and "the impulse to violent aggression" (Douglas, 2008, p. 231). However, he believes that non-biomedical programmes capable of increasing sympathetic feelings can be considered (albeit controversially) as genuine forms of moral enhancement that are at least legitimate (Douglas, 2013, p. 163). On the other hand, Walker (2009, pp. 32-34) proposes a list of virtues (truthfulness, justice, caring) with a genetic basis that could be enhanced in the future, while Hughes (2015) defends a programme of technological enhancement of four interdependent virtues (self-control, gentility, intelligence and positivity).

Let us consider "sympathy", which often appears among the candidate dispositions for moral bioenhancement. There is widespread disagreement in philosophy about the correct way to understand the nature of sympathy and whether it is a necessary condition for morality. As we have seen, for Hume and Smith sympathy is not a disposition, a motive, or a moral emotion, but a mental mechanism that allows one to communicate and share emotions. Moreover, while for Hume its function is very similar to emotional contagion (seeing someone suffering evokes similar emotions in me), for Smith it is closer to what we now call 'empathy', the imaginative ability to project oneself into the shoes of others and experience their emotions (Coplan & Goldie, 2011; Lecaldano, 2013). Persson and Savulescu's definition of empathy seems closer to Smith's conception than to Hume's:

> As we have already highlighted, in our conception, empathy is the ability to vividly imagine what it would be like to be someone else, to think, perceive and feel like someone else. So, as we understand it, empathy does not involve a motivational component. According to this conception, empathy is simply a component of altruism, as we understand it, because we believe that altruism also includes a motivational component of sympathetic concern for the way others feel. (Persson and Savulescu, 2019a, p. 134).

In recent years, critiques of the central role of empathy have come from both the internal front of sentimentality and the external front of rationalism. Jesse Prinz (2011), for example, has accumulated empirical evidence and conceptual arguments to deny that empathy (understood as "a vicarious emotion felt by a person when reflecting on another person's emotion") plays a fundamental role in the formulation of moral judgments, in the development of a moral sense, in the formation of judgments of blame and praise, in deliberative processes, and in moral motivation. Empathy is easily manipulated and characterised by partiality (as Hume also recognised). In some cases, it justifies preferential or "softer" treatment when impartial or "harder" treatment would be more appropriate. At its worst, however, it can encourage attitudes such as nepotism, neglect and moral short-sightedness. The moral harms of empathy can be avoided, according to Prinz, by focusing on other emotions that are essential to moral evaluation, such as anger, disgust, contempt, guilt, pleasure associated with charity, and most importantly, what he calls "concern" defined as "a fellow-feeling that arises when we consider another's plight. [...] Concern is a negative emotion caused by the recognition that someone is in need. […] It is canonically expressed by a knitted brow, akin to worry." (ibid, p. 230). The psychologist Paul Bloom uses similar arguments to defend a rationalist perspective: Empathy, the process that leads to experiencing what the other feels, is marked by enormous limitations, prejudices and biases. It often motivates us to behave in selfish, partial or even violent ways, in direct opposition to altruism. Morality can flourish much better if we rely on people's rational capacities, which allow them to consider the consequences of their actions and the costs and benefits of different options. "Rational compassion" can effectively lead us to care about others and their well-being (Bloom, 2019).

We have presented Prinz and Bloom's arguments not because they are compelling, but only to testify that the debate about the nature of morality is scientifically and philosophically open, and that convergence on some moral dispositions as optimal targets for bioenhancement interventions is not at all apparent. Those who find Prinz and Bloom's critique convincing will hardly be inclined to consider the interventions proposed by Persson and Savulescu and Douglas as examples of genuine "moral enhancement"; indeed, they could even appear as "disenhancements" because they could have disastrous consequences, leading people to behave in antisocial and immoral ways.

The general contrast between sentimentality and rationalism can also be seen in the confrontation between Thomas Douglas and John Harris over moral bio-enhancement. Both philosophers are fierce opponents of conservative arguments against any form of human bio-enhancement. However, Douglas and Harris take opposite positions on moral capacities. As we have seen, Douglas believes that direct manipulation of emotions is a genuine form of moral enhancement, even if it does not improve cognition or reasoning. Harris believes that this approach misunderstands how morality works. For example, it assumes that aversion to certain people because of their gender or ethnicity can be reduced to an instinctive reaction, such as aversion to spiders, and thus underestimates the cognitive content of such attitudes. Racist prejudice is based on beliefs and convictions, so modulating people's emotions would not help prevent racist behaviour. According to Harris, if we want to prevent people from acting racist, we should use traditional or biomedical means to enhance their ability to think rationally and thus correct their beliefs (Harris, 2016, pp. 61-62). Sympathy, empathy, love, concern and other moral emotions are valuable. However, in many cases they are not sufficient to regulate behaviour optimally, and it is in these moments that moral reasoning takes over:

> A moral agent, whatever else she may be, is someone who cares about doing the right thing, someone for whom the difference between right and wrong is important. Such a person will always want to ask him or herself if what feels right is right. And the answer to this question cannot be provided by a second consultation of one's feelings or worse by simply intuiting how one feels about things. (Ibid, p. 113)

Ethical competence, then, is not "being better at being good" but "being better at knowing the good and understanding what is likely to promote the good" (ibid., p. 60). Effective moral enhancements, for Harris, are interventions that do not bypass the person's capacity for judgement and deliberation, that make it more likely that the person will perform good and right actions, and that allow for a more adequate and clear understanding of what the right action is: "It seems to me that moral enhancement, properly so called, must not only make the doing of good or right actions more likely and the doing of bad actions less likely, but must also include the understanding of what constitutes right and wrong action" (ibid., p. 117). Direct intervention in the emotions prevents the individual from thinking rationally and avoids any form of moral reasoning (ibid, p. 81).

For Douglas, Harris's criticism is unconvincing. It may be that in many cases racist behaviour is determined by "false and stereotypical racial beliefs", but this is not enough to rule out the effectiveness of emotional bio-enhancement, given the existence of implicit bias. Even people who claim to be opposed to all forms of racism and discrimination sometimes fall victim to these unconscious biases and, without realising it, are led to act and decide in ways they would not accept (Douglas, 2013, pp. 163-164). Douglas's response again demonstrates the gap between the assumptions of the two proposals. While Harris is convinced that deliberation and rational reflection are necessary conditions for moral behaviour, for Douglas rational mediation is only a sufficient condition, so that in many cases an enhancement that acts directly on emotions and does not involve deliberative intervention implies moral improvement.

The comparison between Douglas and Harris is significant because it illustrates the classic oppositions in ethics and highlights a difference in the various positions for and against moral bio-enhancement that targets feelings, emotions and dispositions. Douglas (2014) notes this by attributing to Harris a concern about the 'superficiality' of emotional bio-enhancement that alters affective and conative mental states: it would induce superficial conformity to moral standards. Hence a lower value in the kind of moral behaviour produced. According to Douglas, it may be less valuable because (a) it would not be motivated by a sense of duty; (b) it would not be derived from a rational deliberative process; (c) the actions would be performed without any effort on the part of the agent; and (d) it would be unreliable. According to Douglas, none of these hypotheses is plausible, because in all cases emotional bio-enhancement facilitates, rather than entirely precludes, rational deliberation. For example, the attenuation of counter-moral emotions, such as tendencies to violence or discrimination, may in many circumstances facilitate the processes of understanding and rational reflection. Moreover, it is not true that the effort we put into deliberation is sufficient to give moral depth to our behaviour.

Douglas raises a real issue, which can be further illustrated by comparing a bio-enhancement intervention with another tool that could be used to change individual behaviour. Many of the printers and photocopiers we use in offices are now preset to print on both sides of the paper, because this limits the amount of paper used. This is an elementary form of 'gentle nudging', a modification of the environment of choice that induces agents to behave in a certain way without compromising their freedom to behave otherwise. In this case, as in others, the push exploits a limitation of human psychology, the status quo bias: we tend to show cognitive inertia, to rely on the given state and to show a natural suspicion of choosing what differs from everyday experience. In the example, no one is forced to print on one side only, but given the cognitive structure of humans, many users will not choose to change the option they feel is already set. The result is that, at the end of the day, many fewer sheets of paper are likely to be used - a desirable outcome from an environmental point of view. However, this does not mean that people who do not choose to change the setting are more aware of the impact of their behaviour on the environment, or that they develop genuine "green virtues", just as in the case of moral bio-enhancement, behaviour is generated that is not linked to genuine development of virtues in the character of the person. Douglas is right to point out that the absence of rational deliberation is not synonymous with a lack of "depth" in behaviour, since there are actions that we perform unconsciously that are in any case related to our moral character, and that the suppression of instinctive impulses and reactions can provide a space for reflection (we will see this aspect more clearly in the last chapter). Nevertheless, any intervention that automatically produces moral behaviour is poorly bound to the person and sounds like mere outward conformity to defined standards. In these cases, it would be necessary to apply several interventions to the same person to ensure that reflection is adequately engaged.

The point, however, is that Douglas understands the effect of moral enhancement in a similar way to De-Grazia: "Behavioural enhancement is highly desirable in the interest of making the world a better place and ensuring a better life for humans and other sentient beings" (DeGrazia, 2014, p. 363). Beyond the specific function of bioenhancement, the intervention aims to produce behaviour that maximises positive consequences in the world. A peculiar way of considering the value of conformity to specific moral standards, as manifested in the actions one takes, emerges in the way Douglas poses the question. This is the modality that Ronald Dworkin (2002, pp. 251-254) has already identified at work in one of the two models that illustrate differences in conceptions of the value of life. Using Dworkin's distinction, it can then be said that proponents of moral bioenhancement tacitly adopt what Dworkin calls the "impact model": the desirability of moral enhancement is that it enables the production of behaviour that has a positive impact on the world. The value of behaviour that respects certain moral standards lies solely in the fact that it eliminates or prevents certain negative states (suffering, coercion, misery, etc.) and/or produces certain positive states (well-being, freedom, prosperity, etc.). In this model, the improvement of moral behaviour is motivated and justified solely by these consequences, regardless of how they are achieved. However, this model can be countered by the "challenge model". In this case, moral improvement is conceived as a performance that requires awareness of the desired outcome and skills that allow it to be integrated into one's whole life. It involves working on oneself, one's relationships and beliefs, and sometimes changing many social relationships. As Dworkin also notes, the challenge model does not deny that part of the value of behaviour lies in the positive consequences it produces. However, it does not reduce it entirely to these, but also emphasises the contribution of the process, in our case the process of reflexively correcting and approving immediate feelings and emotions. On this point, in reality, Persson and Savulescu also recently defended a model of "reflective empathy", which, thanks to the guidance of reason, intervenes in the spontaneous acts of the imagination and produces a "justified altruistic solicitude" and greater motivation to react to injustices (Persson & Savulescu, 2018).

This does not mean accepting a rationalist view of morality. Harris himself seems to recognise that moral education involves established methods:

> bringing children up to know the difference between right and wrong, to avoid inflicting pain or suffering on or doing harm to others; and instilling in them habits of respect for others. These modes of respect include altruism, sensitivity and consideration and perhaps above all of being able to put ourselves in others' shoes so that we not only understand, but imaginatively experience, what it might be like to be on the receiving end of the conduct of others. (Harris, 2016, p. 59)

The space of reflexivity in which we seek to correct feelings and instinctive reactions is not necessarily of a cognitive and rational nature, but can give space to other modalities, such as imagination, according to a perspective we have already seen in Hume and Smith (Lecaldano, 2013, pp. 159-177), but also to practices that take seriously the social and intersubjective nature of morality (we will return to this point in the final chapter). For now, it can be argued that all those interventions that can directly enhance or indirectly facilitate sufficiently broadly understood reflective capacities are effective moral bio-enhancements. This is what is defined in the literature as "procedural moral bioenhancement" or "indirect", since it does not aim to enhance specific dispositions but rather intuitive capacities (Raus et al., 2014, pp. 268- 270; Schaefer, 2015; Paulo,2018; Lavazza & Reichlin, 2019b, pp. 162-163; Schaefer & Savulescu, 2019). This broad conception allows us to share Harris's critique of forms of direct bioenhancement of emotions and moral dispositions that prevent any 'work' on the acquisition and manifestation of moral traits, without being hostile in principle to the possibility of influencing reflexive capacities (while an integrally Kantian position would be much more refractory to this hypothesis (Frammartino & Wilks, 2018)). The space of reflexivity seems essential for preserving the sense of challenge constituted by morality. An important function of this space is not only to produce better effects by modifying behaviour, but also to carry out a moral 'transformation', which requires a process of reflection on one's own character and on the relationships one maintains with the world, other people and sentient beings in general. Every time we are called to choose a change, this takes place; character and experience can provide us with consolidated and reliable indications on which to act.

In other cases, however, reflection means rethinking one's character, beliefs and commitments. To paraphrase Harris, bioenhancement is for the "bad guys" (Harris, 2016, ch. 7); that is, it aims to change the behaviour of those who insist on acting in morally unjust ways; through genetic and pharmacological interventions, it may be possible in the future to achieve an "external" modification that cannot amount to an effective transformation of the self. If the validity of the challenge model is accepted, this result cannot be considered sufficient.

What Do We Need to Enhance? Capacities or People?

Before closing this chapter, there is a further criticism to be made. Even if we accept that some dispositions, such as sympathetic altruism or concern, are necessary and sufficient conditions for morality, it is not certain that strengthening them necessarily leads to moral improvement. In other words, it does not mean that by strengthening a moral disposition or emotion we automatically obtain it. As a result, a morally better person. Douglas himself is very astute on this point. He understands moral bio-enhancement as an intervention aimed at improving, from a moral point of view, the reasons for action that a person possesses. In this way, Douglas remains neutral about how different theories establish what makes a given set of reasons good and what makes a given set of reasons morally better than another. Nor does he make the claim that moral enhancement of motives produces morally better people (Douglas, 2008, pp. 229-230).

A first limitation in this sense of moral bio-enhancement is its "fragmentary" nature. The interventions envisaged isolate a particular positive disposition (empathy, altruism, sense of justice, etc.) or negative disposition (violence, selfishness, discriminatory tendencies, etc.) and propose to strengthen or eliminate it. But the end result is not "more moral" people. In the first place, they bring about a change in a particular part of the human mind without intervening in the subject's motivational and psychological complex, and therefore without guaranteeing that the general tendency to commit immoral acts will continue. We can intervene in an individual's motivational complex and eliminate his or her tendency to discriminate against other individuals who do not belong to his or her ethnic group, but this does not guarantee that the same individual will not behave immorally in other cases, for example by continuing to discriminate against other people on the basis of gender (De Melo-Martín & Seller, 2015, p. 225). Second, according to some authors, proponents of moral bioenhancement underestimate the complexity of moral psychology by reducing it to a single trait (emotional or cognitive) (Hauskeller, 2013, p. 46; Palazzani, 2018, pp. 230-233; Jotterand & Levin, 2019).

A second boundary is set by what we might call 'moral contextuality'. This term refers to a general connotation of moral dispositions that makes them strongly dependent on contextual conditions. In general, we can consider as praiseworthy some virtues (courage, generosity, beneficence, justice, etc.) included in the litanies presented by philosophers such as Aristotle (2005) or Hume (1971a), or the emotions and moral dispositions cited by the proponents of moral bio-enhancement, as well as the condemnation of opposite dispositions and emotions in general. However, a systematic practice of these moral virtues, dispositions and emotions and a systematic abstention from vices, selfish tendencies and anti-moral emotions is not necessarily positive in any situation. Even if a rule is worthy of praise, its indiscriminate reinforcement could cause serious harm. This criticism can take two forms, one more empirical and the other more philosophical.

The empirical version argues that reducing or eliminating negative tendencies (e.g., aggression) and enhancing positive tendencies (e.g., empathy and caring) could lead to morally suboptimal behaviour in situations where being empathetic or less aggressive causes harm or fails to prevent it. Chan and Harris cite the example of Jasper Schuringa, an airline passenger who, on 26 December 2009, attacked and disarmed a hijacker, injuring him and saving the lives of other passengers. If Schuringa had previously been given a pharmacological intervention to reduce aggression, he would have been less likely to act in this situation, with potentially disastrous consequences for the people on the plane. A programme to attenuate or completely eliminate aggression and extreme aversion to some people could have a counterproductive existence (Chan & Harris, 2011, p. 131; Harris, 2016, p. 63). However, even the strengthening of pro-social tendencies could in some cases lead to unacceptable consequences. The strengthening of the sense of justice may lead to cooperation even in situations where it would be morally preferable not to (Hauskeller, 2013, pp. 45-46); for example, when we are asked to cooperate in immoral projects; the strengthening of altruism or the willingness to care for others could lead to an increase in attention to the suffering of others (and the willingness to take an active interest in them) at the expense of freedom and self-care (Manea, 2018, p. 160); the increase in empathy could exacerbate attitudes of exclusion and discrimination towards all people who do not belong to the target group (Ray and Gallegos de Castillo, 2019).

It therefore seems that, in the concrete, the determination of which actions are morally good, just, virtuous, etc., depends strongly on context and on variables that the mechanical action of moral bioenhancement cannot take into account (Wiseman, 2018, pp. 47-51). These observations lead to a philosophical reformulation of this critique. What is lacking in all the cases listed is the ability to contextualise moral attitudes and modulate one's dispositions in relation to the specific demands of a given situation. This attention and sensitivity to detail is the intellectual virtue that Aristotle, as we have seen, called phronesis, 'practical wisdom', the disposition that allows us to grasp the morally relevant properties of a situation and to respond most justly by doing the right thing. Moral bio-enhancement, on the other hand, is insensitive to context and proceeds with "coarse-grained" interventions aimed at indiscriminately strengthening what are considered to be the primary and macroscopic components of morality. As Persson and Savulescu (2019a, p. 138) also acknowledge, certain 'negative' tendencies and emotions must be experienced proportionally in order to play a role in moral life. However, this contextual balancing function cannot consist in the brutal elimination of extremes (low altruism and high aggression) through direct interventions in the biology of dispositions, tendencies and emotions. The "crudeness" is, for some authors, the actual intrinsic limit to any moral bio-enhancement project, as it "failing to enhance people's practical wisdom, cannot really enhance the real virtues" (Huang & Shiu-Hwa Tsu, 2018, p. 202). As we will have the opportunity to explore in Chapter 4, we believe that this conclusion, while highlighting the limitations of the moral bio-enhancement projects we have considered so far, does not apply to other types of interventions that can at least indirectly guarantee real moral improvement by fostering reflexive capacities.

CHAPTER 3

Does Moral Bio-enhancement Negate Our Liberty?

The Meanings of Liberty

One of the most common criticisms of moral bio-enhancement is that it will reduce or eliminate individual freedom. If a large-scale bio-enhancement programme were to take place, individuals would no longer be free to choose and act. In order to better understand the implications of this objection, it is first necessary to understand what it means to be "free", and it is therefore necessary to give some preliminary indications of the descriptive meaning of the term "freedom". We should be clear that we are not concerned here with establishing the value of freedom, but only with clarifying how this term has been interpreted in philosophy.

The concept of 'freedom' can have many meanings. First, we can speak of freedom in terms of both action and choice; we can say that we are free (or not free) to want this or that, and that we are free (or not free) to do this or that. Secondly, we can distinguish between a "metaphysical" and a "political" conception of freedom. In the first case, reference is made to the problem of free will, a question that has been discussed in philosophy for millennia and that has given rise to a rich confrontation in contemporary thought. In the second case, reference is made to the social and intersubjective dimensions of freedom. Free will concerns the relationship between the subject and natural necessity: how can the choice and action of a human person be defined as free when they are subject to multiple determinations of a genetic, neurological, physical nature, etc.? Social freedom, on the other hand, concerns the relationship between the subject and social constraints: under what conditions the choice and action of a human person can be considered free when the person is subject to other subjects or the law of the state (Kristjánsson, 1996; Oppenheim, 2004; Magni, 2005, chap. 2; Magni, 2019, pp. 72-74).

Social freedom defined in this way is relative negative freedom. You are socially free if other subjects do not prevent or force you to choose and act. To take an Aristotelian example, a tyrant has kidnapped my family and orders me to do something vile if I want to see them alive; or, to take a more familiar example, a thief threatens me with a gun and orders me to give him my wallet if I want to live; a person manipulates me into holding false beliefs in order to prevent me from making a particular choice. In these cases, I am not "socially" free because someone else is coercing me and limiting the range of my choices and actions.

To this classical conception of social freedom as negative freedom we can add the theory of freedom as the absence of domination, defended (among others) by Philip Pettit. In short, this theory argues that in order to be free to choose and act, one must have the resources and opportunities to choose according to one's preferences; one must have the possibility of choosing between options beyond the preferred one; and, above all, one must be able to choose the preferred option without this freedom being dependent on the goodwill of another person. According to the last clause, the individual must be independent of the domination of others. This is a much more demanding condition than the classical conception of social freedom. Thus, it is enough to be free if no interference and deliberate obstacles prevent us from other options. It states that not even the availability of the means to choose must depend on the good will of others.

A classic example is the happy slave who wins the sympathy, benevolence and indulgence of his master; but this slave lives in a condition that is certainly more favourable than that of the other slaves; this does not mean that he can be called free. This does not mean that our choices must be completely unrestricted in order to be free: the ability to choose as we wish always depends on a comprehensive system of opportunities determined by the preferences of others and by social norms that guide institutions and organisations that can restrict our choices. To travel by plane, there must be airlines, and there is no general aversion to flying; to buy a house, you need loans from banks, granted according to shared rules and regulations. However, these choices are not (usually) granted by the good will of airline or bank officials, so we do not suffer from the domination of others in these cases. Moreover, the degree of freedom varies with the degree of domination one suffers (Pettit, 2001; 2014).

With regard to free will, however, it is traditionally claimed that a subject is metaphysically free if the following conditions are met: (1) alternative possibilities exist, i.e. the agent can choose and act differently from how he chooses and acts, and (2) the agent exercises conscious control over choices and actions (self-determination). Roughly speaking, there are three main conceptions of free will, distinguished by the different ways in which they conceive of the relationship between freedom and nature: *hard determinism*, *libertarianism*, and *compatibilism*. The first two are incompatible because they argue that determinism and free will are incompatible. If one is true, then the other must be false. For hard determinists, determinism is true and therefore, free will is a mere illusion; for libertarians, given the existence of freedom, determinism must be false. Since it is not possible to convey all the complexity of the comparison between these positions, we will limit ourselves to providing a small map of the prominent positions, referring to the introductory literature on the subject for further information (Magni, 2005; Kane, 2011; De Caro, 2018):

a. *Libertarianism*: Freedom is incompatible with determinism, so in order to have freedom, physical causes can't determine human choices and actions. According to some forms of libertarianism, human actions have a special status that distinguishes them from events that respond to the laws of nature. They can be explained in terms of the agent's intentions, and these explanations are not causal. The absence of natural causality guarantees freedom of will and action. According to other forms of libertarianism, it can be admitted that actions are caused. However, it is possible to identify non-deterministic processes that take place when difficult choices shape the agent's character. Even if the daily choices are determined, it is enough that they are consistent with the person's character. Finally, other libertarians see freedom in the power of the will of rational agents to cause actions without being caused by anything in turn. The salient point of libertarianism, in whatever form, is that the explanation of the genesis of choices and actions is non-deterministic in character: the will is not determined by neural, biological, physical events, etc., to want as it wants. The two conditions of free will, alternative possibilities and self-determination, are fully respected.

b. *Hard determinism*: According to a classical formulation of this concept, every event is determined by past events and the laws of nature, for which there is only one possible future. If determinism is true, then our actions are the consequences of the laws of nature and the events of the distant past. However, what happened in the past is not up to us, and we cannot falsify the laws of nature. Therefore, we have no control over the consequences of the past and the laws of nature (including our present actions), and this would demonstrate that free will is a pure illusion. Since the world is physically structured, neither can fulfil these conditions.

c. *Compatibilism*: There are various forms of compatibilism, a concept supported and defended by Hobbes and Hume. In its most recent formulations, so-called "dynamic" compatibilism (Magni, 2019) focuses on the fact that free will expresses a "power" and interprets this power empirically. To say that X is free to do Y means that X can do Y; that is, there are no external impediments that prevent X from choosing and doing Y, and X has a set of internal conditions that allow it to choose and do Y. The explicit conditions exclude that X is free to choose and do Y, and they interpret this power empirically. The explicit conditions exclude that X is free in cases where he is under the influence of a strong drug because he lacks the ability to choose; he is paralysed because he lacks the ability to act; he lacks suitable options because he lacks the opportunity to choose; he is bound in chains, etc. Therefore, to say that X could have acted differently is to say that X had the ability and the opportunity to choose and act differently. Alternative possibilities and self-determination are conditions that are read empirically. As can be seen from the examples, the assessment of ability and opportunity is independent of the truth or falsity of determinism.

To better understand the difference between the three positions, let's imagine that the agent's life is like a film recorded on a computer file. In one scene, the protagonist makes a certain decision and acts accordingly. As soon as the scene is over, we can use the player to go back to the immediately preceding frame and be sure that if we press play we will see the same scene we have just seen. According to libertarianism, real-life choices don't work like that, because if we could go back in time, the agent, whose will is not determined by anything to choose, might choose differently. We might not see the same scene. For determinists, however, life works like the film: we could go back in time too, but the course of history would not change because we have no control over what happens. Finally, for compatibilists, it can also be admitted that life works like a film. But it is not on the basis of this property that we should decide whether this or that agent was free when he or she made the choice.

This brief overview enables us to examine the discussion of the relationship between moral bioenhancement and freedom.

The Freedom to "Fall"

One of the best known and most discussed formulations of this objection comes from John Harris. Since 2011, Harris has insisted that moral bioenhancement, as understood by Douglas, Persson and Savulescu, is incompatible with preserving the "freedom to fall". This peculiar characteristic of human beings, taken from John Milton's poem *Paradise Lost*, is philosophically an essential element of autonomy and the ability to be self-sufficient: "Autonomy surely requires not only the possibility of falling, but the freedom to choose to fall" (Harris, 2016, p. 59). We are only truly autonomous when we can choose whether to adhere to moral norms and act on the basis of knowledge of what is good and right, or whether to devote ourselves to betraying those norms. The self-determination guaranteed by autonomy also implies responsibility in a twofold sense: we must take care of our deliberate actions and omissions (i.e. the choices we make), and we must be prepared to answer for how we govern ourselves and for the effects that this produces (ibid., p. 96). Both forms of responsibility are possible if, and only if, the decisions are truly ours, that is, if they come from our will. We can influence the world and be accountable for our actions if we are free to choose: "This is why the decision-making process matters; every decision is, in reality, a choice between possible worlds made by that decision" (ibidem). Harris is aware that many forces of a natural (chemical, neurological, biological) and social (pressure, education, etc.) nature are exerted on every decision, including past decisions. For autonomy and responsibility to be given, none of these influences can exclude the will, which must be the cause of the decision in all respects because only in this way will the person be able to justify and explain his actions (ibid., p. 98). "Moral bankruptcy" is the consequence of the divorce between choice and action. Harris is explicit in his belief that freedom, so understood, is a non-negotiable good and not exchangeable even with survival (ibid., pp. 74-75). Moral bio-enhancement compels people to do good and deprives them of the freedom to choose evil. It makes "the freedom to do immoral things impossible, rather than simply declaring them wrong and giving us moral, legal, and prudential reasons to refrain from doing them" (ibid., p. 64).

Harris argues that to be moral agents, we must be free to do good and evil. But it is not only moral bio-enhancement through drugs, neurological interventions or genetic modification that is the enemy of authentic morality. The *God Machine* described by Persson and Savulescu (2012) is an even more disturbing prospect. It is a thought experiment that imagines that in 2050 there will be a device that can monitor people's mental states (thoughts, beliefs, desires, intentions) at any moment and intervene to change them in nanoseconds without them noticing. In this way, the *God Machine* could prevent damage and serious injustice, but would not be activated in the case of minor moral acts such as lying or cheating. According to the authors, the machine leaves people's freedom to do good intact, but takes away their freedom to act immorally. Laws that impose penalties for this type of activity currently make it difficult to carry it out. In contrast, the God Machine would make it virtually impossible to carry it out without the agent being aware of it, but having the illusion of acting freely. In the *God Machine* era:

> It is seen as preferable that would-be murderers "change their minds", rather than an innocent person is killed and then the murderer incarcerated for life. And, the would-be murderer never knows that her intentions have been changed by an authority outside of herself. It seems to her that she has "changed her mind" spontaneously – she experiences a life of complete freedom, though she is not free. Although any intention to kill or rape immediately

> changed, this was put down to the efficacy of moral education. It seemed "from the inside" that she had just developed an aversion to killing an innocent person. And no one was ever killed. (Persson and Savulescu, 2012, p. 413).

In this imagined future, people know of the machine's existence and suspect how it works, but they don't know how often it intervenes. They will be available to undergo massive programmes of this kind without falling under the machine's influence. According to Persson and Savulescu, these people are true lovers of freedom because, in this way, they voluntarily (and therefore freely) choose to be good. Everyone else will be better off without the evil produced by grossly immoral acts, and will still be free to "fall" in less serious ways. Moreover, those who voluntarily choose to connect to the machine will not see their autonomy compromised, for it would be a case of "Ulysses and the Sirens" (ibid., pp. 414-415). Odysseus chose to limit his freedom by being tied to the mast of the ship and instructing his companions not to release him even if he asked them to, so that he could listen to the song of the Sirens without sinking the ship. Similarly, those who choose to connect to the God Machine would deliberately renounce immoral actions in the name of the collective good.

Persson and Savulescu specify that the *God Machine* is not a moral enhancement, which in this future would exist in the usual forms (i.e. biomedical), but a device that prevents immorality (ibid., p. 413). Moreover, they have recently reiterated this point:

> the fact that both GM [*God Machine*] and effective ME [*moral enhancement*] could be sufficient to ensure the same effect it simply does not follow that GM is a form of effective ME. […] although we believe that in principle ME could be so effective that it ensures that human beings do not commit acts that are gravely morally wrong, we have never thought that this effectiveness is a *necessary condition* for a treatment to qualify as ME, nor that the fact that GM possesses this effectiveness is *a sufficient condition* for it qualify as a form of ME. (Persson and Savulescu, 2016, p. 276).

For Persson and Savulescu, the problem is then of an evaluative nature. Even if we assume that in some cases the machine eliminates the freedom to do evil, this loss would be offset by the benefits of the intervention in terms of promoting security, well-being and respect for fundamental rights. This balance justifies the device, even if it violates the individual's freedom to fall.

Although the two authors do not believe that the *God Machine* is a form of moral enhancement, this does not exclude, from Harris's perspective, that both moral bioenhancement and the *God Machine* have ethically problematic aspects for the same reason: they deny the freedom to fall, that is, they prevent you from deliberating and choosing to behave in a (grossly) immoral way. But there are two kinds of problems. First, we need to understand whether, from a descriptive point of view, there really is a loss of freedom in the cases of moral bioenhancement envisaged by Persson and Savulescu, by trying to understand what kind of freedom is at stake and, if this loss actually occurs, whether it is actually justified on the valuation plan.

For example, David DeGrazia (2014, pp. 365-366) denies that moral bioenhancement violates freedom understood as free will, whatever compatibilist or incompatibilist conception we take. Of course, hard determinists won't worry about this threat because they don't believe that free will exists. Libertarians argue that human actions are something different from the events we find in the natural world, where deterministic laws are at work. This independence makes actions completely immune to bioenhancing intervention, which would instead follow the laws of nature. Even indeterministic libertarianism, according to which it is sufficient that individual daily choices, however determined, still derive from an indeterministically formed character, would not be affected by bio-enhancement, which has individual choices as its object. But even for compatibilists, there should be no problem. As long as moral bio-enhancement does not produce effects comparable to paralysis, coercion, or manipulation, and as long as the agent continues to "perform intentional actions that are under his voluntary control" (ibid., p. 366), there would seem to be no lack of freedom in the compatibilist sense. It would only be a further natural determination (Reichlin, 2017, pp. 192-193) because the enhancement would be limited to causing stimulation. However, it would not be a negative influence: according to compatibilism, "acting freely does not require a perfect independence from a causal influence (this is impossible according to this conception), but the right kind of relationship between one's preferences and action, as well as the absence of certain types of conditions that nullify freedom" (ibidem)

However, this objection is not entirely convincing (Danhaer, 2018, pp. 243-246). First, a libertarian might argue that moral bio-enhancement implies a causal determination of the will: a bio-enhanced agent would not be self-determining, but would be pushed to act by a natural causal influence. Furthermore, an indeterminist might argue that if moral bio-enhancement produces actions that are inconsistent with the person's character (as would happen in the case of individuals with a vicious character), then these actions can no longer be considered free. But even on the compatibilist front, where DeGrazia claims to be, there is no salvation. The version of compatibilism that he finds more convincing argues that an action is free if it is autonomous in the following sense:

> A autonomously performs intentional action X if and only if (1) A does X because she prefers to do X, (2) A has this preference because she (at least dispositionally) identifies with and prefers to have it, and (3) this identification has not resulted primarily from influences that A would, on careful reflection, consider alienating'. (DeGrazia, 2014, p. 366).

However, there is no guarantee that an agent undergoing moral bio-enhancement will not find the intervention alienating. A morally good agent is willing to act generously, kindly, etc., because it identifies with its preferences and does not consider that its identification is the product of manipulation, hypnosis, etc. But a morally bad agent undergoing moral bio-enhancement could just as easily feel such alienation. But even if it is conceded that DeGrazia's compatibilism does not suffer from these problems, this does not mean that any form of compatibilism is compatible with moral bioenhancement. For example, an empiricist compatibilist who accepts the "dynamic" conception we presented in the previous paragraph could argue that bioenhancement deprives the agent of the very ability to choose whether to do good or evil, thus depriving it of at least one of the internal requirements for being free, even if it does not affect other capacities or opportunities for choice and action.

Moreover, this is precisely what Harris responds to: the freedom to fall is not the freedom to choose or act differently, but the freedom to 'acquire, or decline to acquire, for reasons, 'values and preferences' that may become stable as they are tested and proven to be effective in, among other things, making the world a better place' (Harris, 2016, p. 81). The same consideration can be advanced even if one accepts the broader conception of reflective capacities introduced in the previous chapter. A moral bioenhancement that nullifies the effect of a person's intuitive capacities deprives the subject of the ability to correct their feelings and emotions. Although the result is significant from the point of view of consequences, the way in which it is obtained is questionable, since it prevents the person from exercising an essential faculty of agency and deprives him of freedom, at least in the context of choices relating to the moral sphere.

The Value of Liberty

Moral bio-enhancement seems incompatible with free will, but why should this concern us? Harris argues that the illusion of freedom generates a "moral bankruptcy", and part of this bankruptcy is that "our responsibility comes from our will, from the fact that we do these things on purpose" (Harris, 2016, p. 95). Therefore, denying the freedom to fall calls into question our nature as responsible beings.

In general, the problem of the value of freedom is addressed by trying to understand whether the balance between the loss of freedom and the realisation of a better world is rational. For example, DeGrazia writes:

> Imagine further that, as a result of MB [*moral bio-enhancement*], there were no more wars or starvation and everyone in the world had access to the basic necessities of life. I, for one, would accept this reduction in freedom across the board if it were necessary for such great improvement in people's moral behaviour and such welcome consequences. (DeGrazia 2014, p. 367).

John Danaher argued that freedom has no intrinsic value, but is a "moral catalyst" because when it is present it can reinforce values already present, whether good or bad. This means that a world without freedom is not necessarily intrinsically bad, and a world in which freedom flourishes is not necessarily intrinsically good, nor is it possible to rank possible worlds in which freedom is present or absent at the expense or benefit of goodness (Danaher, 2018, pp. 241-242). We are not convinced that this is the best way to respond to Harris and those who argue that moral bio-enhancement undermines freedom. Perhaps contrary to Harris's intentions, the idea of 'moral bankruptcy' does not require freedom to be seen as an intrinsic good but as an instrumental good because it allows agents to be held morally responsible for their actions. Perhaps a more convincing way of responding to Harris is to deny the existence of any necessary connection between freedom and responsibility. Peter Strawson (2019), for example, argues that it is not necessary to have metaphysical freedom in order to be held responsible for our actions because the practice of responsibility is based on the way we respond emotionally, with resentment, disapproval, gratitude, approval, and so on, to the good and bad will of others. However, this does not depend on the possession of freedom, but on the absence of conditions that can excuse or exempt the person from their behaviour. Harry Frankfurt (2019) argues that the attribution of moral responsibility does not require alternative possibilities: Bianchi intends to kill Rossi but does not know that Neri, who wishes Rossi dead, has a mind-control device that can make Bianchi carry out the action if he changes his mind (a machine similar to the God Machine). Let's imagine that Bianchi decides whether or not to kill Rossi, but in the end, decides to take the fateful step and carry out the murder. According to Frankfurt, Bianchi has no alternative (if he had decided not to kill him, Neri would have intervened), but he is equally responsible for his actions.

But even accepting the absence of any link between freedom and responsibility is not entirely convincing. First, even if Strawson's responsibility does not imply metaphysical freedom, it does imply something very similar to compatibilist freedom: the integrity of certain reflexive moral capacities is essential for the agent to be morally responsible (Galletti, 2018, pp. 167-180), and these could still be prevented by moral bioenhancement. Second, the device imagined by Frankfurt still conditions Bianchi's actions. Although Bianchi can still be considered morally responsible for what he does when he decides without being influenced by Neri, his reflective capacities are excluded and circumvented when he changes his mind, just as they are for those who suffer the intervention of the God Machine. Furthermore, as Harris notes, the functioning of the device does not allow those on whom it is used to learn from their mistakes, and this has implications for the constitution of moral character and one's agency (Harris, 2016, p. 99).

From this picture it follows that: (1) moral bio-enhancement violates metaphysical freedom and compatibilist capacities; and (2) however, it has a negative impact on human agency, which could also undermine attributions of responsibility. The possibility that moral bio-enhancement also violates social freedom remains to be explored. From this point of view, such an outcome would be very problematic because we believe that the enjoyment of this form of freedom is fundamental. However, this point needs to be further elaborated.

Robert Sparrow (2014a) has pointed out that freedom is also a question of relationships between people and does not end in the metaphysical forms of free will. As noted above, the logical structure of social or political freedom provides for the absence of interference and domination by others. According to Sparrow, there is a disanalogy between moral enhancement achieved by traditional means and moral enhancement achieved by biotechnological means. The former establishes a relationship of equality between the enhancing subject and the enhanced subject. The interventions are justified and defensible by rules that shape the whole project and are accepted (and acceptable) by all involved. The relationship responds to rational demands. Biomedical interventions create a very different relationship because they "operate in an instrumental or technical way" because they undermine the egalitarian relationship between the enhancer and the enhanced, who is treated as an object and not as a subject whose mental states depend entirely on the will of others. According to Sparrow, the freedom that is violated in this case is freedom in the absence of domination. According to Sparrow, the *God Machine* produces a relationship of domination: "the techniques it uses to do so could also be used to control individuals' motivations more generally. The God machine 'dominates' its subjects" (ibid., p. 27).

Sparrow targets Persson and Savulescu's machine, but his critique can be extended to moral bio-enhancement. It could be argued that even moral education can be used to control individual motivations, both moral and general. The problem, then, is not with the medium itself, but with the purpose for which it is used. History contains examples of education being used to achieve greater social control. The real coherence of this criticism is more effectively captured in this passage:

> If somebody else makes it *physically* impossible for me to do what I want to do, then that person exercises a great deal of control over my life. However, if someone manages to make it *psychologically* impossible for me even to *want* anything other than what *that person* wants me to want, then the person's control over me is complete, and this is what moral bioenhancement ultimately seeks to accomplish: a state of complete control, not only over people's bodies, but also over their minds. (Hauskeller, 2017, p. 373).

A state of total control is incompatible with the enjoyment of social freedom. Regardless of the means by which this result is achieved, it creates a morally unacceptable asymmetrical relationship between the enhancer and the enhanced, regardless of the type of action that is prevented. Therefore, it is not only the freedom to fall into danger that is relevant to being moral, but also the social freedom that establishes equal relationships between individuals. This seems essential if we are to think of ourselves as mutually responsible beings. The link between social freedom and responsibility can be clarified by introducing a distinction made famous by P. Strawson. In the essay *Freedom and Resentment*, published in 1968, Strawson points out that our practices of responsibility depend on two perspectives from which we can view other individuals. From the participatory perspective, we see the other as a person engaged in normal intersubjective relations and fully participating in moral practices.

For this reason, it is possible to hold him responsible for the consequences of his actions. If, however, the other person is unable to choose and act because of temporary problems (hypnotic suggestions, intense stress, enormous social pressure, etc.) or permanent problems (immaturity, mental disorders, disorders of moral development, etc.), he or she is seen in a different light. We no longer see her as a subject involved in normal intersubjective relationships, but, in extreme cases, we take an objective perspective and consider her as someone to "cure", "manage", "direct", an individual to be taken in our charge, in a therapeutic sense, using systems of welfare or education (Strawson, 2019, pp. 90-98). Moral bioenhancement suspends all participatory attitudes and considers those who behave unjustly as objects to be manipulated and corrected, rather than as moral agents to be fed inadequate moral dispositions or feelings while remaining full participants in practices of responsibility.

Two objections could be made to this argument. Firstly, some traditional means also have a re-education objective, such as punishment, and therefore take an objective perspective. However, we believe that these measures implemented by the institutions are perfectly acceptable. Secondly, it is not entirely clear why the domination exercised by bioenhancement would be illegitimate, since it simply deprives people of the freedom to commit immoral acts. Freedom, as the absence of domination, is generally regarded as valuable because it protects the possibility of individuals realising their life plans through morally correct or neutral actions. A general response to these objections can be given: in the rule of law there are (at least in principle) sufficient guarantees that in the rehabilitation process the person is treated as a subject and not as a biologically modifiable object according to the wishes of those who enhance. It is precisely this difference that makes the domination exercised by other subjects (private or institutional) over the bioenhanced unacceptable or, in any case, ethically problematic. In the case of bioenhancement, there is no real attribution of the status of agents involved in practices of responsibility to those who behave immorally.

The argument based on the violation of social freedom therefore seems convincing. Nevertheless, it would be necessary to distinguish between bioenhancements that directly enhance emotions and moral dispositions and bioenhancements that directly or indirectly enhance reflective capacities. In the latter case, there does not seem to be a dominant relationship between the parties, since the autonomy and freedom of the enhanced person is guaranteed by the fact that the intervention does not induce motivational and behavioural habits. Furthermore, it also makes a difference whether moral bio-enhancement (as understood by Persson, Savulescu and Douglas) is a paternalistically imposed modification or is voluntarily and freely chosen by the individual who decides to enhance himself. We will return to this point in the next chapter.

CHAPTER 4

Is Moral Bio-enhancement Also Unacceptable?

Moral Progress and Moral Improvement

According to many authors, the motivation that should lead us to opt for moral biotechnology is the presence of evil in the world, produced by human action, which cannot reasonably be eradicated by the means traditionally used in the past, such as individual and collective reflection, moral education and/or socialisation. The biotechnological path is necessitated by this inadequacy and by the need to quickly create conditions that will improve the social world and prevent damage that could lead to the disappearance of human beings.

Moral bio-enhancement, therefore, operates on two levels. The first level is that of moral progress, a collective transition to a state considered more "moral" than the previous one; the second level is that of moral improvement or growth, where the success of the enhancement is measured by the individual who uses it. The two levels are interrelated. If there is no moral improvement at the individual level, it is doubtful whether we can speak of genuine moral progress at the general level. It's not necessary for all people to improve morally in order for moral progress to occur, but a sufficient proportion of them must do so.

The idea of the existence of moral progress has found new life in recent philosophical literature, particularly in relation to reflections on the evolutionary history of morality (Singer, 2011; Musschenga & Meynen, 2016; Buchanan & Powell, 2018; Kitcher, 2021). The theme of moral progress is linked to that of bioenhancement when Persson and Savulescu (as well as Douglas and Walker) argue that traditional means are unable to achieve rapid and adequate progress in morality, and that a biotechnological push is needed. Moreover, this push must be capable of producing more stable transformations, since it intervenes at the biological level. The first thesis can, therefore, be divided into two parts: (1) traditional means do not guarantee moral progress, and (2) biotechnological means can guarantee moral progress. The diagnosis of the current state of humanity and the dangers it faces is taken for granted, even if all do not share it. Harris often repeats that it is very likely that the threats do not come from human wickedness but from human folly (Harris 2016, pp. 3-4, 70-74, 135-136).

Russell Powell and Allen Buchanan have argued that Persson and Savulescu's judgement on the history of morality fails to take account of the fundamental forces that have shaped the natural evolution of behaviour. This judgement rests in part on the premise that commonsense moral psychology is constrained by its own natural history. The "fixed (or highly recalcitrant) nature of human moral psychology" determines that "the most effective means of transcending our inability to extend moral concern beyond the group, including to individuals of future generations, is not sociocultural but biological" (Powell & Buchanan, 2016, p. 243). According to the two philosophers, this premise is accompanied by a Hobbesian conception of morality, according to which human beings are capable of extending moral concern beyond the boundaries of the group only to individuals who are capable of contributing to, or at least not hindering, cooperative relationships. But this is wrong. The recent history of human morality shows that "moral anomalies" are possible, i.e. extensions of consideration that do not follow this pattern. The first example is that of non-human animals, towards which moral attention has increased and which are increasingly included in the moral circle (albeit still with limits), even if they are incapable of cooperation. The second anomaly is the increasing diffusion of the belief in the universality of moral norms, which replaces the criterion of group identification. The third anomaly is the progressive recognition of human rights as fundamental rights that belong to every individual, regardless of their geographical location, and that are based on "cosmopolitan moral principles". Fourth, the emergence of a subject-centred morality that argues for the attribution of moral status even to individuals who do not pose a threat or contribute to cooperation (Buchanan & Powell, 2018, pp. 153-157). Human beings are endowed with the "open normativity of ethics", that is, the "ability to reflect on and review moral norms and to change behaviour, even when doing so not only does not strengthen adaptation but reduces it" (ibid., p. 170). The conclusion is that there is insufficient evidence to support the efficacy of moral bio-enhancement.

At the same time, we have reasonable certainty about the ability of inclusive moral tendencies to deal with violence and environmental degradation. There is no doubt that Buchanan and Powell's theory is fascinating. But it seems overly optimistic about the actual extent of human reflexive capacities to solve all macroscopic problems, and overly pessimistic about the possibilities of moral bio-enhancement. Persson and Savulescu have a good game in retorting that "it is too early to condemn [bio-moral enhancement]; too little research has been made into the matter for either a favourable or unfavourable judgment on its potential effectiveness" and to point out that, although moral bio-enhancement is not a sufficient condition to thwart the threats of catastrophe, it could be a necessary condition to achieve this result (Persson & Savulescu, 2019b, pp. 817-818).

However, Buchanan and Powell's observations help to highlight a limitation of the proponents of moral bio-enhancement. The dimension in which these enhancement programmes are situated is fundamentally *individualistic*. Moral progress appears to be the product of the aggregation of multiple interventions on particular individuals. However, the outstanding moral and social achievements, including the integrative drives mentioned above, are not (in any way) the product of enhanced moral individualities, nor does one need to have enhanced moral psychologies in order to subsequently be able to endorse and follow the norms and values embodied in the social practices and legal systems that have stabilised such achievements. As Nigel Pleasants wrote:

> I aver that it is self-evident, via direct personal reflection, that we citizens who are now enculturated into a social life that upholds principles of gender, sex, sexuality, and racial equality do not denounce and eschew sexism, homophobia, and racism (to the extent that we do) because we have an enhanced moral psychology. We can surely see that recognising the wrongness of, and complying with the legal prohibitions on, slavery, racism, sexism, and homophobia

> involves no specially enhanced or refined sense of trust, co-operation, empathy, altruism, or "morally better motives" on our part. (Pleasants, 2018, pp. 94-95).

The capacity to be moral is essentially social in nature, because it derives from (1) the care (understood in a broad sense) that different people in different social roles take to transmit certain moral attitudes from generation to generation, (2) collective movements that reveal a new moral perspective from which to view the old reality or point to crucial changes and mutations in the social life of people that require institutional recognition, and (3) the attention that institutions pay to creating and supporting appropriate environments for activating individual or group moral behaviour. There is a large empirical and philosophical literature on the situated nature of behaviour and the multiple, unacknowledged environmental influences that can affect individual decisions. This account overcomes a narrowly individualistic conception of moral action and shifts attention from the individual to the context; control over attitudes is not the product of individual will alone, but of competition between personal characteristics and the social environment (Mackenzie & Stoljar, 2000; Christman, 2004; Vargas, 2018). Suppose that the individual's capacity to choose and act is social, both in terms of its emergence and its maintenance. In this case, it becomes essential to design "moral ecologies", environments structured to allow the reflective activity that characterises moral experience (Vargas, 2018, pp. 128- 131; Galletti, 2020).

The relational nature of moral capacities is reflected not only at the public level but also at the individual level. In the broader conception of reflective capacities that we have identified (section 2.4), we have found that the relational, social and intersubjective dimension of moral experience is fully relevant to evaluation and decision making in moral life. As we have said, the exercise of reflexive capacities is not only functional for the resolution of moral dilemmas or for decision making in a particular problematic context, but it is also an engine for the transformation of the self, for the correction of one's character and commitments in order to make room for others and for the moral demands that come from the social world. However, if a social and relational account of agency is accepted, then dialogue, listening and confronting different experiences, stepping out of oneself and returning to it, and changing what is judged inadequate are also crucial. Putting ethics into practice implies a mostly imaginative work, never entirely confined to the private sphere, but nourished by interaction and comparison with the experience of others and with reality. An ethic of care therefore stresses the value of receiving needs and highlights the active part of the commitment to be moral (Botti, 2018).

This way of interpreting what it means to be moral clashes sharply with the reductionist programme of moral bio-enhancement. Focusing exclusively on the biological components of moral behaviour and on individual rules leads to three errors. Firstly, it underestimates the internal complexity of morality, i.e. the possibility that moral judgements and decisions are the product of a number of internal factors (and therefore biological components) and not simply moral dispositions isolated from each other (Jotterand 2016). Second, it completely excludes the relational factor from the picture, and the fruitfulness of thinking of the moral agent as part of a stratified relational system that does not replicate forms of social determinism but fosters the relational resources necessary for effective morality. Third, it too often equates moral improvement with simple make-up: to use a perhaps crude analogy, it sometimes seems that moral improvement is the equivalent of changing one's hair colour. Again, this account fails to take account of the transformative processes of morality. If moral enhancement really wants to produce moral improvement in people, and not just consequences that would be judged utilitarianly positive, it must take into account the work on the self and character that moral experience implies. However, this does not seem possible in the way that moral bio-enhancement is understood by the authors with whom we have dealt.

Do Morally Acceptable Bio-enhancements Exist?

Having reached the end of our journey, we might ask whether any kind of moral bio-enhancement is unacceptable. We have already mentioned that bio-enhancements that facilitate the exercise of reflective capacities might be considered legitimate. We will see an example of this kind at the end of this section.

We also stressed that moral bio-enhancement violates social freedom because it introduces a relationship of domination. Such a critique presupposes that the intervention is *imposed*, that there is a person or institution that exercises dominion over the individual by forcing him or her to undergo bioenhancement. Moreover, Persson and Savulescu affirm in their book that tangible results in the fight against terrorism and global warming can only be achieved by restricting individual freedoms and rethinking the ethical, political and legal structure of liberal democracies. On the coercive nature of the moral bio-enhancement programme, Persson and Savulescu take an ambiguous position. In their book they are not unbalanced, while in other writings they have argued more explicitly that there are no good reasons to reject the coercion of bio-enhancement (Persson & Savulescu, 2008, p. 174; Persson & Savulescu, 2012; Savulescu, 2020). Other authors have defended these interventions as top-down engineering projects of moral capacities that some public institutions should impose on citizens in more or less hidden ways (Gordon, 2016; Crutchfield, 2019; Crutchfield, 2021). Such an approach seems problematic, especially when the justification for infringing on citizens' individual freedoms seems problematic in terms of the benefits that might result. As Bublitz (2016, p. 100) wrote:

> The mere idea that the minds of citizens are a legitimate target for governmental intrusions is, by itself, unsettling. The central challenge for MBE proponents is to establish the legitimacy of governmental programs that exert pressure on individuals, that incentivise use of MBE in large parts of the population, effectively influencing opinion formation of the populace [...], and of course those that eliminate 'morally defective mental states' [...] without informed consent or in those notoriously contested grey areas of voluntariness such as incarcerated offenders.

It would be different if moral bio-enhancement were voluntary, although recommended. This solution, coordinated with explicit guarantees preventing any inequalities, would make it possible to encourage the use of drugs or the use of genetic modifications without restricting the social freedom of citizens (Rakić, 2014; 2021). We believe that the solution of voluntary bioenhancement is reasonable. Hauskeller (2017, p. 374) argues that the voluntary form of enhancement would be equivalent to a self-imposed act of slavery. In fact, it would not be unlike signing a contract in which freedom is consciously surrendered: a

Kantian contradiction on the formal level and a self-defeating or self-destructive choice on the substantive level. Mill himself condemned voluntary enslavement as an act contrary to freedom. But this does not seem to be a valid objection. Voluntary bio-enhancement could be likened to an allegory of "Ulysses and the Sirens": like Ulysses, who chooses to be tied to the mast of the ship in order not to fall for the sirens' deceptive seduction, those who morally choose bio-enhancement could choose to limit their autonomy in the short term in order to enjoy it more in the future. Even if this were a fundamental restriction of freedom, it would be entirely justified if, from the person's point of view, moral bio-enhancement is a legitimate means of self-improvement.

However, anyone claiming the superiority of voluntary over coercive moral bio-enhancement must be aware of two limitations. The first is a problem that even Persson and Savulescu (2019b, p. 819) recognise because it is common to both forms of enhancement: those who should voluntarily resort to moral bio-enhancement must already be willing to improve themselves morally, and this creates a vicious circle. This problem is common to both forms of bio-enhancement. It is obvious in the case of voluntary bio-enhancement because the totally evil or selfish person will have no inclination to take drugs to become "moral". Voluntary choice of this kind is more likely to be made by people who suffer from weak wills and recognise the right course, but have stronger desires that lead them not to conform their behaviour to what they believe to be morally right behaviour. In the case of coercive moral bio-enhancement, the link is less clear, but the governments tasked with imposing interventions on the population are made up of people with limited moral psychologies. Moreover, if such officials do not have a genuine moral inclination, or have not voluntarily chosen to be bio-enhanced, they may be tempted not to decide to enhance the population if it conflicts with their other interests. Let's take the example of a politician who contributes to increasing citizens' fear of immigration, on which his electoral consensus is based, and who knows that a collective bio-enhancement programme would reduce general distrust of foreigners. The option of improving the moral dispositions of the population would be unattractive to him, because it would have the defect of hindering his personal interest.

Moreover, as Wiseman (2016, pp. 202-204) points out, if moral bio-enhancement is indeed effective, we should distinguish between cases in which behaviour requires and justifies coercive intervention (such as sadistic paedophile rapists) and other cases in which moral bio-enhancement must be voluntarily chosen. (Note, however, that Wiseman is a strong critic of moral bio-enhancement, but in this case, by proposing a case-by-case analysis, he seems to support a perspective similar to that imagined in the *God Machine* scenario: coercive intervention to correct the personality of those who commit heinous crimes, and free choice for all morally suspect but non-serious behaviour, such as lying).

We therefore defend the moral right of people to use whatever means they consider most appropriate for moral development, whether biotechnological or traditional, as long as they are sufficiently safe, even if we believe that the prospect of direct intervention in emotions and dispositions does not produce effective moral improvement (though it does produce morally appreciable consequences all things considered). We end this section with an example of procedural or indirect bioenhancement that is likely to already be in place, and which we consider to be perfectly acceptable. This is the use of drugs such as Ritalin on children suffering from attention deficit and hyperactivity (Galletti, 2016; Galletti, 2019). The fact that they are children does not matter. Coercive interventions on children are generally and *prima facie* justifiable because they cannot decide for themselves. However, as we shall see, it is essential to involve the recipients of this bioenhancement by strengthening their perspective.

Commonly known as ADHD, this syndrome is characterised by an inability to sustain attention and concentration and to perform tasks, particularly in a school environment, and a tendency to exhibit behaviours that indicate poor motor control and a low propensity to inhibit responses. This lack of self-control can lead to actions that are harmful to the individual (e.g. crossing the road without looking or making hasty decisions on important matters) or, less harmful, simply annoying others (social intrusiveness). In general, there are two types of intervention to treat ADHD: cognitive-behavioural training, treatment with drugs containing psychostimulants such as methylphenidate (commonly known by the brand name Ritalin), or multimodal interventions. These drugs have an onset of action of 8-10 hours and are generally well tolerated in terms of safety, although they are not without adverse effects, ranging from mild to severe.

Some argue that ADHD is a social construct rather than a deficit that has obvious biological markers and was 'invented' to serve economic and social interests in the growing inability to manage 'abnormal' behaviour that deviates from what is statistically and legally considered 'normal' behaviour. ADHD behaviour would therefore be a simple variation on the normal and physiological behaviour of school-age children, disguised as a disorder, and the suffering of the current population diagnosed with ADHD would not be due to this disorder, but to an altered perception of social spaces such as schools, and to a chronic lack of resources that makes it difficult to reconcile a particular environment with actions that are potentially destructive of its peaceful order. Other more moderate positions recognise the dependence of the manifestation of symptoms on the social context, without denying the reality of the disorder. Both anti-realist and constructivist positions share the idea that there are cases in which children show symptoms and are damaged by such symptoms. Doctors, teachers and parents disagree about the adequacy of the diagnosis of ADHD. Therefore, it is at least possible that some healthy children are treated with medication. The recurring objection is that this prevents children from learning to take responsibility for their behaviour and makes them feel that they are being controlled by chemicals rather than by their own will.

Empirical data are scarce, but some research by the psychologist Ileana Singh shows that these children do not perceive themselves as having been transformed into unconscious automatons controlled only by "chemical impulses" (Singh, 2007; Singh & Keller, 2010; Singh, 2013). For example, children interviewed using special questionnaires reported feeling as if they were in a "middle" position, i.e. in a state where they could choose to behave for better or worse. The drug treatment allowed them to meet moral demands by weakening or eliminating the impulse to act and leaving room for deliberation. The drugs, therefore, allow "children to assess whether a particular situation justifies an aggressive response. [...] the most important function of medication is not to 'tell' a child what the right action is, but to enable a child to make a mental space for deliberation. It is this capacity for reasoning, even in the face of peer aggression, that constitutes what we might call good character" (Singh, 2013, p. 363). Rather than perceiving drugs as a threat to their sense of moral agency, some children see them as a mediating factor that enables them to better interact with the regulatory expectations of their environment.

It could be argued that drug treatment does not improve children's moral capacities because it merely produces compliance with a regulatory standard. Children think they are making decisions and acting independently, but what they are doing is simply responding passively to environmental demands. This objection may not be sufficient to dismiss psychostimulants as immoral, but it helps to consider an important concern. The potential normalising effect highlights the need to provide opportunities for children to reflect and challenge norms. The use of psychostimulants leaves room for autonomy. It does not turn children into automatic machines, but allows them to distinguish between an impulsive violation of a norm and a challenge to the norm. When a subject challenges a norm, he is exercising his will because he is taking responsibility for rejecting the normative requirement. The second problem concerns the acceptability of the means used to comply with the rules. As Singh writes:

> If a majority of children are not victims of stimulant drugs, then they can be engaged to help uncover threats to agency or to authenticity, and they can be constructively supported to protest normative expectations and the accompanying tools, as appropriate. Children also need to be able to openly discuss the value of medication in relation to their capacity for moral decision-making and their capacities to meet standards of behaviour demanded of them in a given ecological niche. (Ibidem, p. 364).

It is therefore important to involve children in the assessment of both expectations and use of stimulant medication. Furthermore, recent studies show how children actively deal with ADHD. For example, Honkasilta, Vehmas, and Vehkakoski (2016) argue that young people with ADHD construct their identity as moral agents in at least three ways. The assumption behind all these modes of self-understanding is that children do not try to adapt their identities to psycho-medical discourses and do not passively identify with the behavioural disorder, but accept ADHD as belonging to them and mobilise the diagnosis of the disorder to build a particular practical identity. Children may perceive

ADHD as (1) an excuse that relieves them of moral guilt, (2) an underlying disorder that they can and should control, or (3) a justification because they say they are resisting social stigmas and a rigid categorisation of the self. Children in the second and third categories claim to be in control of their condition and want to be seen as responsible agents, but the third category also offers another perspective. Children who see ADHD as a justification tend to challenge the normative expectations of their environment and shape their practical identity in opposition to demands to conform to a moral standard.

The empirical evidence seems to suggest that we can only assess whether the use of psychostimulants has harmful effects on children on a case-by-case basis. The drug cannot be a "mechanical act" (a pill to solve a problem). It must be part of a complex strategy that actively involves the child's point of view in order to modulate the appropriate response to their behaviour, to continue with pharmacological intervention or to change the regulatory expectations of the environment.

In these cases, can psychostimulant drugs be considered a form of moral bio-enhancement? They do not directly affect moral cognition, moral motivation or moral dispositions, but *indirectly* facilitate the exercise of the individual's intuitive capacities, allowing them to act more autonomously. The children Singh interviewed helped create a reflective mental space in which they could consider the demands of their environment, shape their moral dispositions and feelings, and decide whether to meet those demands. The bio-enhancing use of psychostimulants is morally acceptable in the first instance because deeper and broader research is needed on the effects of drugs on moral agency and identity. The final judgement on the acceptability of a given technology depends on its beneficial or harmful consequences. The potential harms and side effects must be carefully considered in order to rule out the possibility that the long-term use of this treatment will be detrimental to health and self-perception. Having made these clarifications, the moral bio-enhancement guaranteed by these substances allows you to exercise greater control over yourself, your deliberations and your actions (Pugh, 2014), if accompanied by adequate first-person involvement of the child. It is conceivable that the possibility of "moral growth" of individuals cannot be achieved by pharmacological intervention alone but will continue to require a broader educational and social effort. It is precisely this synergy that should be the primary objective of a responsible introduction of moral bio-enhancement.

The integration of biotechnological and traditional means must also aim to maintain a critical sense of moral norms. We believe that this point is crucial both to limit the effect of *superficial conformity* to norms and values and to avoid the effect of *moral conformity* to a single system of norms and values, thus avoiding the use of enhancement techniques (technological or *humanistic*) that threaten moral perspectives and public debate. In the model of the reflexive ethics of challenge, the possibility of individual and collective moral improvement is essentially linked to the comparison and experience of difference, to dialogue and the recognition of different ways of life and moral demands, even those far removed from those to which one is accustomed. This would be impossible or much more difficult if the introduction of moral bio-enhancement consisted only in the use of a means of social control or a tool capable of producing behaviour that is only outwardly moral or considered more virtuous according to a single standard of evaluation.

BIBLIOGRAPHY

Agar N. (2010). *Humanity's End: Why We Should Reject Radical Enhancement*, MIT Press, Cambridge (MA).

Agar N. (2014). *Truly Human Enhancement. A Philosophical Defense of Limits*, MIT Press, Cambridge (MA).

Almeida M., Diogo R. (2019). "Human Enhancement: Genetic Engineering and Evolution", in *Evolution, Medicine, and Public Health*, (2019)1, pp. 183-189.

Amodio D., Devine P. (2006). "Stereotyping and Evaluation in Implicit Race Bias: Evidence for Independent Constructs and Unique Effects on Behavior", in *Journal of Personality and Social Psychology*, 91(4), pp. 652-661.

Amodio D., Harmon-Jones E., Devine P. (2003). "Individual Differences in the Activation and Control of Affective Race Bias as Assessed by Startle Eyeblink Response and Self-Report", *Journal of Personality and Social Psychology*, 84(4), pp. 738-753.

Aristotle. 1999, *Etica Nicomachea*, (ed.) C. Natali, Laterza, Roma-Bari.

Axelson R.D. et al. (2010). "Assessing Implicit Gender Bias in Medical Student Performance Evaluations", *Evaluation & the Health Professions*, 33(3), pp. 365–385.

Balistreri M. 2020, Superumani. Etica e potenziamento umano, Espress Edizioni, Torino (2nd ed.).

Balistreri M. 2022, *Il bambino migliore*, Fandango, Roma.

Bloom P. 2019, *Contro l'empatia. Una difesa della razionalità*, Liberilibri, Macerata (Original Edition 2016).

Borenstein J., Arkin R. (2016). "Robotic Nudges: The Ethics of Engineering a More Socially Just Human Being", in *Science and Engineering Ethics*, 22(1), pp. 31-46.

Bostrom N., Sandberg A. 2009. The Wisdom of Nature: An Evolutionary Heuristic for Human Enhancement, in J. Savulescu, N. Bostrom (eds.), *Human Enhancement*, Oxford University Press, Oxford, pp. 375-416.

Botti C. 2018, *Cura e differenza. Ripensare l'etica*, LED, Milano.

Brownstein M., Saul J. (eds.). (2016). *Implicit Bias and Philosophy: Volume 2, Moral Responsibility, Structural Injustice, and Ethics*, Oxford University Press, Oxford.

Bublitz C. (2016). "Moral Enhancement and Mental Freedom", *Journal of Applied Philosophy*, 33(1), pp. 88–106.

Buchanan A. (2011). (2011). *Beyond Humanity? The Ethics of Biomedical Enhancement*, Oxford University Press, Oxford.

Buchanan A., Powell R. (2018). *The Evolution of Moral Progress. A Biocultural Theory*, Oxford University Press, Oxford.

Carlana M. (2019). "Implicit Stereotypes: Evidence from Teachers' Gender Bias", *The Quarterly Journal of Economics*, 134(3), pp. 1163–1224.

Casebeer W.D. 2005, *Natural Ethical Facts: Evolution, Connectionism, and Moral Cognition*, MIT Press, Cambridge (MA).

Casebeer W.D., Churchland P.S. 2003, "The Neural Mechanisms of Moral Cognition: A Multiple-Aspect Approach to Moral Judgment and Decision-Making", *Biology and Philosophy*, 18, pp. 169-194.

Casebeer W.D., Churchland P.S. 2003, "The Neural Mechanisms of Moral Cognition: A Multiple-Aspect Approach to Moral Judgment and Decision-Making", *Biology and Philosophy*, 18, pp. 169-194.

Chan S., Harris J. (2011). "Moral Enhancement and Pro-social Behaviour", in *Journal of Medical Ethics*, 37(3), pp. 130–131.

Christen M. et al. (eds.) 2013, *Empirically Informed Ethics: Morality between Facts and Norms*, Springer, Cham.

Christman J. (2004). "Relational Autonomy, Liberal Individualism, and the Social Constitution of Selves", in *Philosophical Studies*, 117(1/2), pp. 143–164.

Colzato L.S., Arntz F.E. 2017, Ritalin, in L.S. Colzato (eds.), *Theory-Driven Approaches to Cognitive Enhancement*, Springer, Cham, pp. 71-80.

Colzato L.S., Mourits R. (2017). Modafinil, in Colzato (ed.), *Theory-Driven Approaches to Cognitive Enhancement* cit. pp. 83-93.

Coplan A., Goldie P. (eds.). (2011). *Empathy. Philosophical and Psychological Perspectives*, Oxford University Press, Oxford.

Corbellini G., Sirgiovanni E. 2013, *Tutta colpa del cervello. Un'introduzione alla neuroetica*, Mondadori Università, Milano.

Crockett M.J. 2014, "Moral Bioenhancement: A Neuroscientific Perspective", *Journal of Medical Ethics*, 40(6), pp. 370-371.

Crockett M.J. et al. (2010). "Serotonin Selectively Influences Moral Judgment and Behavior through Effects on Harm Aversion", in *Proceedings of the National Academy of Sciences*, 107(40), pp. 17433–17438.

Crutchfield P. (2019). "Compulsory Moral Bioenhancement Should Be Covert", in *Bioethics,* 33(1), pp. 112–121.

Crutchfield P. (2021). *Moral Enhancement and the Public Good*, Routledge, New York.

Dasgupta N. (2013). "Implicit Attitudes and Beliefs Adapt to Situations: A Decade of Research on the Malleability of Implicit Prejudice, Stereotypes, and the Self- Concept", in *Advances in Experimental Social Psychology*, 47, pp. 233–277.

Danaher J. (2018). Moral Enhancement and Moral Freedom: A Critique of the Little Alex Problem, in M. Hauskeller, L. Coyne (eds.), *Moral Enhancement: Critical Perspectives,* Cambridge University Press, Cambridge, pp. 233–250.

Darby R.R., Pascual-Leone A. (2017). "Moral Enhancement Using Non-invasive Brain Stimulation", in *Frontiers in Human Neuroscience*, 11(77), pp. 1–10.

De Caro M. (ed.) 2018, *La logica della libertà*, Mimesis, Milano.

DeGrazia D. (2014). "Moral Enhancement, Freedom, And What We (Should) Value In Moral Behaviour", in *Journal of Medical Ethics*, 40(6), pp. 361–368.

De Melo-Martín I. (2018). The Trouble with Moral Enhancement, in Hauskeller, Coyne (ed.), *Moral Enhancement: Critical Perspectives* cit., pp. 19-33.

De Melo-Martín I., Salles A. (2015). "Moral Bioenhancement: Much Ado about Nothing?", in *Bioethics*, 29(4), pp. 223-232.

Douglas T. (2008). "Moral Enhancement", in *Journal of Applied Philosophy*, 25(3), pp. 228–245.

Douglas T. (2013). "Moral Enhancement via Direct Emotion Modulation: A Reply to John Harris", in *Bioethics*, 27(3), pp. 160–168.

Douglas T. (2014). "Enhancing Moral Conformity and Enhancing Moral Worth", in *Neuroethics*, 7(1), pp. 75–91.

Dovidio J.F. et al. (2002). "Why Can't We Just Get Along? Interpersonal Biases and Interracial Distrust", in *Cultural Diversity and Ethnic Minority Psychology*, 8(2), pp. 88-102.

Dworkin R. (2002). *Sovereign Virtue*, Harvard University Press, Cambridge (MA).

Earp B.D., Sandberg A., Kahane G., Savulescu J. (2014). "When Is Diminishment a Form of Enhancement? Rethinking the Enhancement Debate in Biomedical Ethics", in *Frontiers in Systems Neuroscience*, 8, pp. 1–8.

Edmonds D. 2014. *Uccideresti l'uomo grasso? Il dilemma etico del male minore*, Raffaello Cortina, Milano.

Faust H.S. 2008, "Should We Select for Genetic Moral Enhancement? A Thought Experiment Using the Moralkinder (MK+) Haplotype", in *Theoretical Medicine and Bioethics*, 29, pp. 397-416.

Frammartino Wilks A. 2018, Kantian Challenges for the Bioenhancement of Moral Autonomy, in M. Hauskeller, Coyne (eds.), *Moral Enhancement: Critical Perspectives* cit., pp. 121-143.

Frankfurt H. 2019, Possibilità alternative e responsabilità morale, in De Caro (ed.), *La logica della libertà* cit., pp. 115-127 (ed. or. 1969).

Galletti M. 2011, La grammatica morale universale. Forme e limiti della competenza morale umana, in M. Galletti, S. Vida (eds.), *Indagine sulla natura umana. Itinerari della filosofia contemporanea*, Carocci, Roma, pp. 124-148.

Galletti M. 2016, "Forme di miglioramento morale. L'uso di farmaci psico-stimolanti tra terapia e miglioramento", in *Bioetica. Rivista interdisciplinare*, 14(4), pp. 1-22.

Galletti M. 2018, *Reciprocamente responsabili. La responsabilità morale tra naturalismo e normativismo*, ETS, Pisa.

Galletti M. (2019). "'Enhancement or Dehancement?' The Use of Psychostimulant Drugs on Children with ADHD" in *Notizie di Politeia*, 35(1), 43–51.

Galletti M. 2020, Il luogo dell'ignoranza nell'etica: privilegi, responsabilità e pregiudizi impliciti, in A. Verza, S. Vida (eds.), *Postfemminismo e neoliberalismo*, Aracne, Roma, pp. 75 98.

Giubilini A., Savulescu J. 2018. "The Artificial Moral Advisor. The "Ideal Observer" Meets Artificial Intelligence", in *Philosophy & Technology*, 31(4), pp. 169- 188.

Gordon J.-S. 2016, "Should Moral Enhancement Be Compulsory?", in *Ethical Perspectives*, 23(2), pp. 277- 306.

Greely H.T. 2021, *CRISPR People. The Science and Ethics of Editing Humans*, MIT Press, Cambridge.

Habermas J. 2002, *Il futuro della natura umana. I rischi di una genetica liberale*, Einaudi, Torino (Original Edition 2001).

Haidt J. (2001). "The Emotional Dog and Its Rational Tail: A Social Intuitionist Approach to Moral Judgment", in *Psychological Review*, 108(4), pp. 814–834.

Harris J. (2007). *Enhancing Evolution. The Ethical Case for Making Better People*, Princeton University Press, Princeton (NJ).

Harris J. (2016). *How to Be Good. The Possibility of Moral Enhancement*, Oxford University Press, Oxford.

Hauskeller M. 2013, *Better Humans? Understanding the Enhancement Project*, Acumen, Durham.

Hauskeller M. (2017). "Is It Desirable to Be Able to Do the Undesirable? Moral Bioenhancement and the Little Alex Problem", in *Cambridge Quarterly of Healthcare Ethics*, 26(3), pp. 365–376.

Hauskeller M., Coyne L. (eds.). 2018, *Moral Enhancement: Critical Perspectives*, Cambridge University Press, Cambridge.

Huang P., Shiu-Hwa Tsu P. (2018). Biomedical Moral Enhancement in the Face of Moral Particularism, in Hauskeller, Coyne (eds.), *Moral Enhancement: Critical Perspectives* cit., pp. 189-208.

Hughes J.J. 2015, "Moral Enhancement Requires Multiple Virtues. Toward a Posthuman Model of Character Development", in *Cambridge Quarterly of Healthcare Ethics*, 24(1), pp. 86-95.

Hume D. 1971a, Ricerca sui principi della morale, in E. Lecaldano, E. Mistretta (eds.), *Opere*, Laterza, Roma-Bari, volume 2 (Original Edition 1751).

Hurlemann R. et al. (2010). "Oxytocin Enhances Amygdala- Dependent, Socially Reinforced Learning and Emotional Empathy in Humans", in *Journal of Neuroscience*, 30(14), pp. 4999-5007.

Jotterand F., Levin S.B. 2019. "Moral Deficits, Moral Motivation and the Feasibility of Moral Bioenhancement", in *Topoi*, 38(1), pp. 63-71.

Jotterand F. (2016). Moral Enhancement, Neuroessentialism, and Moral Content, in F. Jotterand, V. Dubljević (eds.), *Cognitive Enhancement. Ethical and Policy Implications in International Perspectives*, Oxford University Press, Oxford, pp. 42–56.

Juengst E.T., Moseley D. (2019). Human Enhancement, in E.N. Zalta (ed.), *Stanford Encyclopedia of Philosophy,* 25 May 2019, https://plato.stanford.edu/entries/enhancement/.

Kane R. (ed.). (2011). *The Oxford Handbook of Free Will*, Oxford University Press, Oxford (2nd ed.).

Kant I. 1995a, Critica della ragion pratica, in P. Chiodi (ed.), *Scritti morali*, UTET, Torino (ed. or. 1788).

Kant I. 1995b, Fondazione della metafisica dei costumi, in *Scritti morali*, (ed.) P. Chiodi, UTET, Torino (ed. or. 1785).

Kitcher P. (2021). *Moral Progress*, Oxford University Press, Oxford.

Krakowski M. (2003). "Violence and Serotonin: Influence of Impulse Control, Affect Regulation, and Social Functioning", *Journal of Neuropsychiatry and Clinical Neuroscience*, 15, pp. 294–305.

Kristjánsson K. (1996). *Social Freedom: The Responsibility View*, Cambridge University Press, Cambridge (MA).

Kuepper Y. et al. (2010). "Aggression-Interactions of Serotonin and Testosterone in Healthy Men and Women", in *Behavioural Brain Research*, 206(1), pp. 93-100.

Lara F. (2021). "Why a Virtual Assistant for Moral Enhancement When We Could have a Socrates?" in *Science and Engineering Ethics*, 27(42), pp. 1–27.

Lavazza A., Reichlin M. (eds.). 2019a, "Moral Enhancement", *Topoi,* 38(1), pp. 1-151.

Lavazza A., Reichlin M. 2019b, Postfazione. Inadatti a cosa? Il dibattito recente sul potenziamento morale "tecnologico", in Persson I., Savulescu J., (eds.). *Inadatti al futuro. L'esigenza di un potenziamento morale*, Rosenberg & Sellier, Torino, pp. 159-167.

Lecaldano E. 2013, *Simpatia*, Raffaello Cortina, Milano.

Levy N. et al. (2014). "Are You Morally Modified? The Moral Effects of Widely Used Pharmaceuticals", in *Philosophy, Psychiatry, & Psychology,* 21(2), pp. 111- 125.

Mackenzie C., Stoljar N. (2000). *Relational Autonomy: Feminist Perspectives on Autonomy, Agency, and the Social Self*, Oxford University Press, Oxford.

Magni S.F. 2005, *Teorie della libertà. La discussione contemporanea*, Carocci, Roma.

Magni S.F. 2019, *L'etica tra genetica e neuroscienze. Libero arbitrio, responsabilità, generazione*, Carocci, Roma.

Manea T. (2018). Enhancing Care, in Hauskeller, Coyne (ed.), *Moral Enhancement: Critical Perspectives* cit., pp. 145–163.

Mehlman M.J., Berg J.W., Juengst E.T, Kodish, E. 2011, "Ethical and Legal Issues in Enhancement Research on Human Subjects", in *Cambridge Quarterly of Healthcare Ethics*, 20, pp. 30-45.

Musschenga A.W., Meynen G. (eds.). 2017, *Moral Progress, in Ethical Theory and Moral Practice*, 20(1).

Olson M.A., Fazio R.H. 2006, "Reducing Automatically Activated Racial Prejudice through Implicit Evaluative Conditioning", in *Personality and Social Psychology Bulletin*, 32(4), pp. 421-433.

Oppenheim F.E. 2004. "Social Freedom: Definition, Measurability, Valuation", in *Social Choice and Welfare*, 22(1), pp. 175-185.

Palazzani L. 2018, "Biopotenziamento morale: argomenti per una valutazione critica", in *Rivista di filosofia del diritto*, 7(2), pp. 221-240.

Paulo R. (2018). Moral-Epistemic Enhancement, in Hauskeller, Coyne (ed.), *Moral Enhancement: Critical Perspectives* cit., pp. 165–188.

Payne B.K. 2005, "Conceptualizing Control in Social Cognition: The Role of Automatic and Controlled Processes in Misperceiving a Weapon", *Journal of Personality and Social Psychology*, 81, pp. 181-192.

Persson I., Savulescu J. (2008). "The Perils of Cognitive Enhancement and the Urgent Imperative to Enhance the Moral Character of Humanity", in *Journal of Applied Philosophy*, 25(3), pp. 162-177.

Persson I., Savulescu J. (2012). "Moral Enhancement, Freedom, and the God Machine", in *The Monist,* 95(3), pp. 399-421.

Persson I., Savulescu J. (2013). "Getting Moral Enhancement Right: The Desirability of Moral Bioenhancement", in *Bioethics*, 27(3), pp. 124-131.

Persson I., Savulescu J. (2016). "Enharrisment: A Reply to John Harris about Moral Enhancement", in *Neuroethics*, 9(3), pp. 275-277.

Persson I., Savulescu J. (2018). "The Moral Importance of Reflective Empathy", in *Neuroethics*, 11(2), pp. 183–193.

Persson I., Savulescu J. 2019a, *Inadatti al futuro. L'esigenza di un potenziamento morale*, Rosenberg & Sellier, Torino (Original Edition 2012).

Persson I., Savulescu J. (2019b). "The Evolution of Moral Progress and Biomedical Moral Enhancement", in *Bioethics,* 33(7), pp. 814-819.

Pettit P. (2001). *A Theory of Freedom: From the Psychology to the Politics of Agency*, Polity Press, London.

Pettit P. (2014). *Just Freedom. A Moral Compass for a Complex World*, Norton & Co., New York.

Pleasants N. (2018). Would Aristotle Have Seen the Wrongness of Slavery If He Had Undergone a Course of Moral Enhancement?, in M. Hauskeller, L. Coyne (eds.), *Moral Enhancement: Critical Perspectives* cit., pp. 87–107.

Powell, R., & Buchanan, A. (2016). The Evolution of Moral Enhancement. In S. Clarke, J. Savulescu, T. Coady, A. Giubilini & S. Sanyal, *The Ethics of Human Enhancement: Understanding the Debate* (pp. 239–260). Oxford: Oxford University Press.

Prinz J. (2011). "Against Empathy", in *Southern Journal of Philosophy*, 49(1), pp. 214–233.

Pugh J. (2014). "Enhancing Autonomy by Reducing Impulsivity: The Case of ADHD", in *Neuroethics*, 7(3), pp. 373–375.

Rakić V. (2014). "Voluntary Moral Enhancement and the Survival-at-any-cost Bias", in *Journal of Medical Ethics*, 40(4), pp. 246–250.

Rakić V. (2021). *How to Enhance Morality*, Springer, Cham.

Raus K. et al. (2014). "On Defining Moral Enhancement: A Clarificatory Taxonomy", in *Neuroethics*, 7(3), pp. 263-–273.

Ray K., Gallegos de Castillo L. (2019). "Moral Bioenhancement, Social Biases, and the Regulation of Empathy", in *Topoi*, 38(1), pp. 125-133.

Ray K., Gallegos de Castillo L. (2019). "Moral Bioenhancement, Social Biases, and the Regulation of Empathy", in *Topoi*, 38(1), pp. 125-133.

Rueda J., Lara F. (2020). "Virtual Reality and Empathy Enhancement: Ethical Aspects", in *Frontiers in Robotic and AI*, 7, pp. 1–18.

Sandel M.J. 2008, *Contro la perfezione. L'etica nell'età dell'ingegneria genetica,* Vita e Pensiero, Milano (Original Edition 2007).

Savulescu J. (2020). *Mandatory Morality: When Should Moral Enhancement Be Mandatory?* https://blog.practicalethics.ox.ac.uk/2020/11/mandatory-morality-when-should-moral-enhancement-bemandatory/.

Savulescu J., Sandberg A., Kahane G. (2011). Well-being and Enhancement, In R. Ter Meulen, J. Savulescu, G. Kahane (eds.), *Enhancing Human Capacities*, Wiley-Blackwell, Oxford, pp. 3–18.

Savulescu J., Maslen, H. (2015). Moral Enhancement and Artificial Intelligence: Moral AI?, in J. Romportl, E. Zackova, J. Kelemen (eds.), *Beyond Artificial Intelligence. The Disappearing Human-Machine Divide*, Springer, Cham, pp. 79–95.

Schaefer G.O. 2015. "Directs vs. Indirect Moral Enhancement", in *Kennedy Institute of Ethics Journal,* 25(3), pp. 261-289.

Schaefer G.O., Savulescu J. 2019. "Procedural Moral Enhancement", in *Neuroethics*, 12(1), pp. 73-84.

Scheele D. et al. (2014). "Opposing Effects of Oxytocin on Moral Judgment in Males and Females", *Human Brain Mapping*, 35(12), pp. 6067-6076.

Shalvi S., De Dreu C.K.W. 2014, "Oxytocin Promotes Group-Serving Dishonesty", in *Proceedings of the National Academy of Sciences*, 111(15), pp. 5503–5507.

Singer, P. 2011, *The Expanding Circle. Ethics, Evolution, and Moral Progress*, Princeton University Press, Princeton (NJ) (Second ed.).

Singh I. (2007). "Clinical Implications of Ethical Concepts: Moral Self-Understandings in Children Taking Methylphenidate for ADHD", in *Clinical Child Psychology and Psychiatry*, 12(2), pp. 167–182.

Singh I. (2013). "Not Robots: Children's Perspectives on Authenticity, Moral Agency and Stimulant Drug Treatments", *Journal of Medical Ethics*, 39(6), pp. 359–366.

Singh I., Kellher K. J. (2010). "Neuroenhancement in Young People: Proposal for Research, Policy, and Clinical Management", in *American Journal of Bioethics Neuroscience*, 1(1), pp. 3-16.

Songhorian S. (2020). *Etica e scienze cognitive*, Carocci, Roma.

Sparrow R. (2014a). "Better Living Through Chemistry? A Reply to Savulescu and Persson on 'Moral Enhancement", in *Journal of Applied Philosophy*, 31(1), 23–32.

Sparrow R. 2014b,(2014b). "Egalitarianism and Moral Bioenhancement", in *American Journal of Bioethics*, 14(4)– pp. 20-28.

Strawson P.F. 2019, Libertà e risentimento, in De Caro (ed.), *La logica della libertà* cit., pp. 85-114 (Original Edition 1968).

Terbeck S. et al. 2012,(2012). "Propranolol Reduces Implicit Negative Racial Bias", in Psychopharmacology, 222, –p. 419-424.

The President's Council on Bioethics. 2003, *Beyond Therapy. Biotechnology and the Pursuit of Happiness*, Washington, D.C.

Vargas M.R. 2018, The Social Constitution of Agency and Responsibility. Oppression, Politics, and Moral Ecology, in K. Hutchison, C. Mackenzie, M. Oshana (eds.), *Social Dimensions of Moral Responsibility*, Oxford University Press, Oxford, pp. 110-136.

Walker, M. (2009). "Enhancing Genetic Virtue: A Project for Twenty-First Century Humanity?" in *Politics and the Life Sciences*, 28(2), pp. 27-–47.

Walter N.T. et al. (2012). "Ignorance Is No Excuse: Moral Judgments Are Influenced by a Genetic Variation on the Oxytocin Receptor Gene", in *Brain and Cognition*, 78(3), pp. 268–273.

Westbrook A. et al. (2020). "Dopamine Promotes Cognitive Effort by Biasing the Benefits versus Costs of Cognitive Work", in *Science*, 367(6484), pp. 1362–1366.

Wiseman H. 2016,(2016). *The Myth of Moral Brain: The Limits of Moral Enhancement*, MIT Press, Cambridge (MA).

Wise (2018).. 2018, The Sins of Moral Enhancement Discourse, in Hauskeller, Coyne (ed.), *Moral Enhancement: Critical Perspectives* cit., pp. 35-–58.

Wood M. et al. (2009). *A Test for Racial Discrimination in Recruitment Practice in British Cities,* Department for Work and Pensions, London.

Zak P.J. 2012, *The Moral Molecule. The Source of Love and Prosperity*, Dutton, New York.

Zak P.J. et al(2007).7, "Oxytocin Increases Generosity in Humans", in *PLoS One*, 2(1), pp. 1-5.

Zarpentine C. (2013). "'The Thorny and Arduous Path of Moral Progress': Moral Psychology and Moral Enhancement", in *Neuroethics*, 6(1), pp. 1–1-153.

9786156696397.